College English
Self-adaptive Reading

新指南大学英语
自主阅读 ④

总主编 **李华东**

主　编 **夏甘霖**

副主编 **陆月华　徐文姣**

编　者 **郝韵涵**

U0368735

清华大学出版社

北京

内容简介

　　《新指南大学英语自主阅读》1—4册是根据教育部最新发布的《大学英语教学指南（2020版）》，为我国普通高等院校大学生量身打造的一套自主阅读教材。

　　本套书每册包括8个单元，每个单元包含视频导入、语言输入、阅读技巧和语言输出4大部分：导入部分精选主题相关视频，扫码即看，并设计有理解性和思辨性练习；语言输入部分由Banked Cloze、Long Passage和Short Passages 3个板块组成，所选篇章均借助语言数据技术，标注了篇章长度（NW）、语言难度（GL）、语言学术性（AWL percentage）和关键词（Keywords）等数据，练习与大学英语四、六级考试题型完全接轨；1—4册共32个单元的阅读技巧板块有机融入，构成完整的阅读技能训练体系；语言输出部分聚焦学术词汇训练和写作训练。

　　本套教材兼顾基础级别目标（第1、2册）和提高级别目标（第3、4册），适合我国普通高校一、二年级大学生使用。

图书在版编目（CIP）数据

　　新指南大学英语自主阅读.4 / 李华东总主编；夏甘霖主编. — 北京：清华大学出版社,2021.8（2024.8重印）
　　ISBN 978-7-302-58496-4

　　Ⅰ.①新… Ⅱ.①李… ②夏… Ⅲ.①英语—阅读教学—高等学校—教材 Ⅳ.①H319.37

　　中国版本图书馆CIP数据核字(2021)第121304号

责任编辑：刘细珍
封面设计：子　一
责任校对：王凤芝
责任印制：宋　林

出版发行：清华大学出版社
　　　　　网　　址：https://www.tup.com.cn，https://www.wqxuetang.com
　　　　　地　　址：北京清华大学学研大厦A座　　　邮　编：100084
　　　　　社 总 机：010-83470000　　　　　　　　邮　购：010-62786544
　　　　　投稿与读者服务：010-62776969，c-service@tup.tsinghua.edu.cn
　　　　　质量反馈：010-62772015，zhiliang@tup.tsinghua.edu.cn
印 装 者：大厂回族自治县彩虹印刷有限公司
经　　销：全国新华书店
开　　本：185mm×260mm　　印　张：12.25　　字　数：225千字
版　　次：2021年10月第1版　　　　　　印　次：2024年8月第5次印刷
定　　价：59.00元

产品编号：092136-02

《新指南大学英语自主阅读》是根据教育部最新发布的《大学英语教学指南（2020 版）》（以下简称"《指南》"），借助语言数据技术，为我国普通高等院校大学生量身定制的一套自主阅读教材。

一、教材特色

本套教材务求体现以下特色：

1. 依据《指南》编写，针对基础和提高级别

《指南》指出，"大学英语教学目标分为基础、提高、发展三个级别"，并对三个级别的阅读理解能力进行了描述。本套教材针对基础和提高两个级别研发，能覆盖绝大多数普通高等院校大学生，满足他们提高英语阅读理解能力的需求。

2. 借助语言数据技术，助力自主阅读

为帮助学习者了解自己的水平，掌控自己的阅读进度，本套教材所选阅读篇章均标注了篇章语言数据，具体如下：

- 篇章长度（number of words，简称"NW"）：便于自学者了解自己的阅读速度（速度 = 篇章长度 / 阅读时间）。

- 语言难度（Flesch-Kincaid Grade Level，简称"GL"）：GL 数值等于美国学生年级，比如 GL 为 8 的篇章从难度上适合美国八年级学生阅读。近10 年来我国主要英语考试的英语阅读篇章 GL 数值分别为：高考英语 8.3左右，大学英语四级考试 10.8 左右，大学英语六级考试 11.8 左右。

- 语言学术性（Academic Word List percentage，简称"AWL percentage"）：采用 Coxhead 于 2000 年研发的学术词表，计算每篇阅读中学术词汇比例，便于自学者提高自身学术英语阅读能力。依据 Coxhead 的研究，学术语篇的 AWL percentage 比例为 9.9% 左右。

- 关键词（keywords）：每篇文章提供 3 个关键词，便于自学者在阅读前大致了解文章内容。

按照克拉申（Krashen）的输入假设（Input Hypothesis），制约语言习得的

主要因素是语言输入，而最佳的语言输入是稍稍超出学习者现有语言能力的输入。借助上述语言数据，自学者可以了解自己的阅读水平和阅读喜好，从而选择稍稍超出自己现有阅读水平的篇章进行阅读，进而有针对性地提高自己的语言能力。

3. 实施主题教学模式，提高词汇复现率

本套教材选择与中国大学生学习和生活密切相关的话题，每个单元围绕同一个话题展开，在加大学习者知识广度和深度的同时，提高词汇复现率，并穿插视频观看（Viewing）和写作（Writing）环节，有效将学生的认知性词汇（passive vocabulary）转化为复用式词汇（active vocabulary）。

二、教材架构

本套教材包括 4 册书，书后均附视频脚本和练习参考答案。每册主题和语言技能安排如下表：

级别	主题	阅读技能设置
1	大学生活、教育、时尚、饮食、情感、旅行、性格、社交	以《指南》规定的基础级别目标阅读技能为主
2	爱情、成长、大学校园文化、生活方式、感情与交往、合作与冲突、创业、职业规划	
3	课外生活、语言的力量、健康与美容、跨文化交际、数据时代、创新、人工智能、基因技术	以《指南》规定的提高级别目标阅读技能为主
4	职业规划、工作选择、财务管理、旅行、环保、因特网与生活、工作地点选择、新教育模式	

三、单元设置

本套教材每册包括 8 个单元，每个单元包含 4 大部分共 7 个板块，其中语言输入部分的练习形式采用大学英语四、六级考试的 4 种题型，具有极强的针对性。具体单元设置如下表：

模块构思	板块设置	板块描述
导入	Viewing（视频导入）	通过与单元主题相关的精选视频导入本单元的主题，引发学生阅读兴趣

	Banked Cloze（集库式完形填空）	以集库式完形填空形式拓展学生的词汇量和语篇理解能力
语言输入	Long Passage（长篇速读）	以信息匹配形式提高学生的快速阅读（skimming and scanning）能力
	Short Passages（短篇细读）	通过多项选择题（multi-choice questions），全面提高学生的阅读理解能力，如掌握主旨（main idea）、找寻细节（details）、进行推断（inference）、词语释义（paraphrase）、判断态度（attitude）等能力
阅读技巧训练	Reading Skills（阅读技巧训练）	根据本单元阅读篇章特点，总结阅读技巧，并进行适度拓展练习，训练学生掌握这些阅读技巧
语言输出	Academic Words in Use（学术词汇训练）	精选本单元出现过的学术词汇，以集库式完形填空形式训练学生，让他们学会使用这些学术词汇，提高学生学术阅读能力，能用英语作为媒介学习学术内容
	Writing（写作训练）	通过写作训练复习本单元所学内容。训练题型有三种：一是大学英语四、六级考试作文题型；二是读后续写；三是单元内容小结

四、适用对象

本套教材适合我国普通高校一、二年级大学生使用，兼顾基础级别目标（第 1、2 册）和提高级别目标（第 3、4 册），并适度关注了学术词汇的学习。

五、教材使用建议

本套教材主要用于学生课下自学，可以与大学英语主干教材配套使用，也可以单独使用。

六、编写团队

本套教材总主编为上海海事大学李华东教授，第 1—4 册分别由温州商学院、内蒙古大学、浙江传媒学院和上海政法学院的教研团队编写。丛书编写方案由上海海事大学团队研发，主要成员包括朱莉雅、刘慧丹、陈园园、郝韵涵等。感谢清华大学出版社刘细珍老师在丛书策划、编写和成书过程中给予的大力支持。

本套教材系国家社会科学基金项目（17BYY103）部分成果。

由于编写时间紧，本套教材可能存在错漏和不妥之处，请教材使用者批评指正。

《新指南大学英语自主阅读》编写团队

2021 年 5 月

Contents

Contents

Contents   vii

Unit **1** Career Planning

Viewing

The Fantasy, the Ideal, and the Reality of Career Exploration

About the video clip

This video clip introduces the process of job exploration, which is hard, messy and complicated.

Understanding the video clip

The following statements describe John's job-hunting experience, but they are out of order. Please put them into the correct chronological order.

1. John is happily employed as a Senior Patent Agent at a biotech company.

2. John narrowed his choices of career to three, namely, a management consultant, a medical science liaison, and a medical writer.

3. John met with a career counselor and took a self-assessment test.

4. In order to be a patent agent, John started reading and talking to people again.

5. John got no interviews though he had applied for numerous jobs.

6. John took a regulatory writing course, which cost him 2,500 dollars.

7. John gave up the choices of being a consultant and medical science liaison successively.

8. John followed the suggestion of taking the patent bar and finally succeeded.

Further thoughts

Nowadays, more and more young people are leaving school and unable to find jobs after graduation. What do you think are the reasons? What suggestions will you offer to the job-hunters?

Reasons for unemployment	Suggestions for job-hunters
1.	1.
2.	2.
3.	3.
...	...

Banked Cloze

There is a passage with ten blanks. You are required to select one word for each blank from the list of choices given in a word bank following the passage. Read the passage carefully before making your choices. Each choice in the bank is identified by a letter. Please write the corresponding letter for each item in the blanks. You may not use any of the words in the bank more than once.

A Great New Job Is Just a Click Away[1]

NW: 255　GL: 8.1　**AWL percentage:** 5.06%　**Keywords:** Internet; job; unemployment

The Internet has made it much easier to find 1.____, but the number of candidates applying has quadrupled.

Our new Zoom reality has taught us all the importance of a(n) 2.____ Internet connection. It isn't just crucial to the way many of us do our current jobs; it's also how we find new ones.

In the old days, a peasant could only expect their cousin's cousin to know about a decent job in a(n) 3.____ village. But the interweb makes it much easier to find vacancies offering the type of work we're after. That should mean better matches, with more workers finding the right jobs, so they stick at them, become more 4.____ and earn more. That's

---

1　From The Guardian website.

been the view of economists, with research on Norway broadband rollout, for example, finding that it led to higher wages and significantly lower 5._____.

But a new study on Germany challenges this, finding no 6._____ on the quality of job matching from the recent 7._____ of high-speed Internet. The problem? Fast Internet means we all get a better idea of what jobs are out there, and the unemployed do find work more 8._____. But the ease of applying online results in a quadrupling of 9._____ for every job. This problem has probably grown as online recruitment has become the norm. We should have seen this coming. The Internet 10._____ teaches us that we can have too much of a good thing and that the peasants always knew a bigger haystack made it harder to find the needle.

A) neighboring	B) candidates	C) productive
D) challenging	E) vacancies	F) Internet
G) decent	H) unemployment	I) quietly
J) repeatedly	K) effect	L) impact
M) quickly	N) peasants	O) spread

Long Passage

You are going to read a passage with ten statements attached to it. Each statement contains information given in one of the paragraphs. Identify the paragraph from which the information is derived. You may choose a paragraph more than once. Each paragraph is marked with a letter. Please answer the questions by writing the corresponding letter after the statements.

What Every College Student Should Be Doing for Career Success[2]

NW: 873   GL: 9.9   AWL percentage: 6%
Keywords: college student; career success; planning

A   There are different types of college students: the ones who spend their years locked away in the library, the ones who leave everything to the last minute, the ones who spend more time socializing than studying, the ones who split their time between work and the classroom, the ones who do either one of the above things and the ones who try to do them all.

B   With all these experiences college comes with, preparing for the future from the first day may not be a priority. And by this, I mean the post-graduation life. I know

---

2   From Forbes website.

I didn't start thinking about it until my sophomore year. In retrospect, I should've probably started planning sooner. But since I can't undo the past, I can only share what I've learned and help someone in the situation I was in.

C   If possible, every college student should start planning for the future early. This means being involved on campus and staying in the know of what's happening, networking with professors and going after professional experiences—this is all in addition to studying and acing your classes of course. Doing this can be the difference between many job offers by the time it's graduation season and a long period of unemployment or underemployment. As a college student, you want to stay on top of what needs to be done to create a positive outcome.

D   McGraw-Hill Education's[3] Future Workforce Survey revealed some interesting (and in some cases, troubling) statistics about recent graduates.

E   **College graduates don't feel well-equipped to face the real world.** Only 4 in 10 US college students feel very or extremely prepared for their future careers. Women were less confident in their career readiness. Many reported feeling like their college experience did not provide the critical skills they need to transfer into the workforce, such as solving complex problems (43%), resume writing (37%), interviewing (34%) and job searching (31%).

F   **There's a gap between student and employer perceptions.** 77% of students reported feeling confident in their professionalism, work ethic, teamwork and collaboration skills, while employers felt less enthusiastic—according to the recent NACE[4] Job Outlook Study. In fact, only 43% of them feel recent grads are proficient in these areas.

G   **More experience helps with confidence and career readiness.** More than half of the students surveyed said increased access to internships and other professional experiences would have helped them feel better prepared.

H   You may find these findings scary or motivating (I hope it's the latter). While for the most part, they point to a grim post-college reality, there is something you can do for a better outcome. Yes, you can take control from this point forward and make the most out of your college experience—for better job prospects and career opportunities after graduation. Use these tips to formulate your action plan:

I   **Take advantage of your campus career resources.** Are you a regular visitor of

---

3 McGraw-Hill Education: 麦格劳·希尔教育公司是一家对学校提供教育软件、服务和内容的美国公司。由 James H. McGraw 和 John A. Hill 于 1888 年成立。

4 NACE: National Advisory Committee on Electronics （美国）国家电子顾问委员会

your college career center? If not, you're part of the 40-something percent of students surveyed who reported not taking advantage of it. And if that's the case, you should start. From job fairs, career advisors to resume support and internships, there are so many campus career resources available. As a student, you need to be proactive in finding and using them.

J　　It wasn't until the start of my sophomore year that I discovered my school's career center. I took advantage of the many different workshops they offered (resume building, cover letter writing, interviewing, networking, etc.) and it was a game-changer for my early career. From this I gained the skills to land more than four internships and volunteer at a nearby university—all before my senior year. This helped me feel so much more prepared for the real world after graduation.

K　　**Actively look for professional opportunities.** Whether it be a season job, internship or volunteer gig[5], take every opportunity you come across to develop the skill set you'll need in the future. Finding these jobs will often require a proactive approach combined with patience, so carve out some time to do the work. Connect with other students to form a supportive network where you'll encourage each other.

L　　In this highly competitive landscape, come up with creative ways to stand out in the job search. Maybe you'll develop an app to apply for a tech internship or send a physical toolbox of your resume for a job at Home Depot[6] (yes, this actually happened). Keep in mind, it doesn't have to be something so out of the ordinary in order to get hired. Bringing some originality and creativity to the job search certainly helps your chances though.

M　　**Create your own opportunities.** Don't limit yourself to internships or traditional jobs to acquire the experience you'll need when you join the workforce. Especially if these opportunities aren't coming your way. In this digital age, anyone can start a successful venture with a few clicks and a good WiFi connection. Whether you start a blog, launch a photography business or take an online coding/marketing course, use part of your free time to give yourself opportunities with the same gains (more experience). This is the key to not only practicing leadership, managing your time, connecting with new people, but also (and most importantly) honing a set of skills.

1.　More than half of employers think college graduates are not proficient in professionalism and collaboration skills.　☐

5　volunteer gig: 临时的志愿者工作

6　Home Depot: 美国家得宝公司，全球领先的家居建材用品零售商，业务遍布美国、加拿大、墨西哥和中国等地区，连锁商店数量达 2234 家。

2. Internships and professional experiences are regarded as helpful to build up confidence. ☐

3. Students should make full use of the resources available on campus. ☐

4. Some college students value studying than anything else. ☐

5. The present digital age can help students start up their own businesses. ☐

6. Besides studying and acing classes of course, college students should often communicate with professors. ☐

7. About 60% of college students feel unprepared for their future career, especially female students. ☐

8. Students are encouraged to develop the skill set for the future by doing season jobs. ☐

9. I feel regretful that I didn't plan my career earlier. ☐

10. Although post-college reality is stern, you can prepare as early as possible for a better outcome. ☐

Short Passages

There are two passages in this part. Each passage is followed by some questions or unfinished statements. For each passage there are four choices marked A, B, C, and D. You should decide on the best choice and mark the corresponding letter.

Passage one

How to Build a Successful Business[7]

NW: 383   GL: 10.2   AWL percentage: 5.88%   Keywords: business; management; flywheel

If you are looking for a flourishing industry, consider management books. Since starting its column, Bartleby[8] has been buried alive by examples of the genre. Get it right, and there is a lot of money to be made. *Good to Great* by Jim Collins was one of the most successful; all told him he has sold more than 10m books. His latest is a monograph, *Turning the Flywheel*, which builds on a concept from his most famous work.

The idea is that of a virtuous circle, where success in one era leads to success in another, in a self-sustaining fashion. Mr. Collins starts with Amazon, where low prices attract customer visits, which attracts third-party sellers, allows the company to expand,

---

7 From The Economist website.
8 Bartleby: 美国一个以收藏经典参考书、诗歌、小说为主的网站，提供大量免费的电子图书。

growing its revenues faster than its costs, and allowing prices to be lowered even further. Something similar happens at Vanguard, the fund management group, which offers low-fee tracking funds, attracting customers, and allowing costs to be cut even further.

Both of the above examples are really cases of exploiting economies of scale. But other models are available. In the case of Intel, the flywheel started with high-performance chips that customers were willing to pay high prices for. Those high profits were invested in research and development, allowing Intel to produce the next generation of chips before its competitors caught up.

Mr. Collins argues that this approach can work outside the corporate sector, citing a school which hired exceptional teachers, thereby improving results and creating a reputation as a good place to teach, enabling more top teachers to be hired.

The secret, he emphasizes, is eternal vigilance. "To keep the flywheel spinning, you need to continually renew, and improve with each component," he writes.

All this is quite convincing and Mr. Collins avoids the sin of many management books, being neither incomprehensible nor inconsequential. Still, a lot of businesses may feel that the problem lies in setting up the flywheel in the first place. If you are a small business with low volumes, your cost ratio will be quite high, so it is difficult to deliver low prices. And if you take over a struggling school or hospital, you may want to hire the best teachers and doctors, but they usually don't want to come, and you don't have the budget to hire them.

1. **Which of the following statements about Jim Collins is NOT true?**

    A. He is the author of the book entitled *Good to Great*.

    B. He puts forward the concept of "flywheel".

    C. He is the founder of Amazon.

    D. He is a successful entrepreneur.

2. **"Flywheel", according to Jim Collins, is _____ .**

    A. a heavy wheel in a machine that helps to keep it working smoothly

    B. a heavy wheel used to regulate the engine's rotation

    C. a facility in the amusement park

    D. a virtuous circle, where success in one era leads to success in another

3. Which of the following is NOT the example of exploiting economies of scale?

    A. Intel.

    B. Amazon.

    C. Vanguard.

    D. Taobao.

4. What is the key to keeping the flywheel spinning?

    A. Low prices of products.

    B. Continuous renewal and improvement of each component.

    C. High prices of products.

    D. Investing more money to research.

5. Why is it hard for small businesses to copy this model of flywheel?

    A. Because small businesses are short of money.

    B. Because small business owners have no insight.

    C. Because the cost ratio is quite high.

    D. Because small businesses lack core technology.

Passage two

How to Make Work More Enjoyable[9]

NW: 405　GL: 8.5　AWL percentage: 5.45%　Keywords: work; enjoyable; working hours

Do you enjoy your job? Only 13% of employees feel engaged in their jobs, according to a Gallup[10] survey of global workers. That is a pretty depressing statistic, considering how much of our lives we spend on our jobs.

But every problem creates a marketing opportunity and there are plenty of authors eager to sell books telling us how our working lives can be improved. In *The Joy of Work: 30*

9　From The Economist website.

10 Gallup: 盖洛普咨询公司。这是全球著名的商业市场研究和咨询服务机构，创立于 1935 年，公司运用科学的方法调研和分析，并据此为客户提供营销和管理咨询，从而帮助客户取得卓越的商业和学术成果。

Ways to Fix Your Work Culture and Fall in Love with Your Job Again, Bruce Daisley offers a range of sensible, and jargon-free solutions.

The tone is very similar to the book *You Don't Have to Be Crazy at Work* which I wrote up for the column last year. Don't work so hard that you lose sleep. Keep meetings short and limit them to small groups of people. Disconnect from your phone for a while. Have a break and take a walk. Interact socially with your colleagues in a relaxed atmosphere and you are more likely to cooperate fruitfully on a task. Give other people space to think and be creative.

There is an irony in some of this sound advice. Mr. Daisley works for Twitter, one of the great distractions from worker efficiency. Modern technology has had a terrible impact on the length of the effective working day. An American study found that 60% of professionals were remaining connected to work for 13.5 hours every weekday and another five hours at weekend. A study by Tom Jackson of Loughborough University[11] suggests we are interrupted by work emails around 96 times in an eight-hour day, or once every five minutes. The smartphone is an electronic Big Brother, straight out of George Orwell.

Another feature of modernity is the dreaded open-plan office, which may lead to reduced face-to-face communication. The author cites a study showing that people in open-plan offices also take more sick days. They are also interrupted every three minutes, on average, and it can take another eight minutes for their full concentration to return. By which time, of course, they have been interrupted again.

At this point, workers may nod their heads sadly in agreement. The problem is that employers expect them to reply to their emails promptly, to be contactable at all times and stuff them in open-plan offices because they are a lot cheaper. There is not a lot the average Joe[12] or Joanna can do in response.

1. **The fact that only a small percentage of employees feel engaged in their jobs, though depressing, has _____.**

    A. created a marketing opportunity

    B. made many employees quit their job

    C. caused many employees to sell books

    D. made many companies go bankrupt

---

11 Loughborough University: 英国拉夫堡大学

12 an average Joe: 俚语，指"普通人"，一般指男性。后面的 Joanna 指普通的女性。

2. **Which of the following is NOT the suggestion that the writer gave to the employees?**

    A. Don't work too hard.

    B. Keep meetings short.

    C. Interact with colleagues in a relaxed atmosphere.

    D. Always use mobile phones to connect with colleagues.

3. **In Paragraph 4, the writer cited some statistics to show _____.**

    A. Twitter is one of the great distractions of efficient work

    B. modern technology has had a terrible impact on working efficiency

    C. employees are often interrupted by emails while working

    D. employees are not concentrated on their work

4. **Open-plan office has the following advantages EXCEPT that _____.**

    A. employees can be contactable at all times

    B. employees can reply to their boss's emails promptly

    C. employers can save money in office management

    D. there are less distractions for employees

5. **Which of the following statements about work is NOT true?**

    A. Without work, life would be boring.

    B. It's impossible for people to love work every single day.

    C. People work just for their livelihood and no one really loves it.

    D. Some meetings are pointless and unnecessary.

Reading Skills

Text Marking

When you are reading a text that contains many facts and opinions, it is helpful to mark the important facts and opinions so that they stand out and can be used for reviewing and remembering the material.

1 What to mark in a text

You should select and make visually memorable only the most important information or ideas:

- the topic of the passage

- the thesis statement, if the thesis is directly stated

- signals for the overall pattern of the passage

- the main idea

- the details that support the thesis or main idea, including key dates or names

- ideas that seem to differ from what you already know or have read about

- terms or points that are difficult to understand

2 How to mark a text

The following is a list of different kinds of marking that are useful. You should try out all of these techniques and then decide which ones work best for you. Experienced readers develop their own personal style of marking, usually a combination of various techniques.

- underlining (in pencil)

- circling or making a box around words or phrases

- drawing lines or arrows from one part of the text to another

- writing a key word, date, or name in the margin

- making a star or arrow in the margin beside an important point

- making a question mark or exclamation point to express your reaction

- numbering points in series

Exercises

Please read the Long Passage "What Every College Student Should Be Doing for Career Success" again and complete the outline with proper words after marking the text.

Different types of college students: _____1_____ types.

Preparing for the future should be _____2_____.

Some problems with college students:

    a. College graduates don't feel _____3_____ to face the real world.

    b. There's a gap between student and _____4_____.

    c. More experience helps with confidence and _____5_____.

Tips on formulating students' action plan:

    a. Take advantage of your campus career _____6_____.

    b. Actively look for professional _____7_____.

    c. _____8_____ your own opportunities.

THINK

Academic Words in Use

Fill in the blanks in the following sentences with the appropriate words provided in the box below. Change the form of the words if necessary.

measure	accomplish	compete	recruit	harsh
support	proportionate	employment	flourish	convince

1. The club members did agree to modify their _____ policy.

2. A(n) _____ effect should become apparent about three years after widespread implementation.

3. Very quickly, she learned to appreciate life rather than to judge everything so _____.

4. A vastly _____ burden falls on women for childcare.

5. No _____ words could ever compensate for the pain of being separated from her children for 10 years.

6. _____ may be an underlying cause of the rising crime rate.

7. His function is vital to the _____ of the agency's mission.

8. Our cause is _____ and has no lack of successors.

9. Graduates have to fight for jobs in a highly _____ market.

10. There is _____ evidence of a link between exposure to sun and skin cancer.

Writing

For this part, you are allowed 30 minutes to read the following paragraphs and continue writing to make it a well-structured article. You should write at least 180 words but no more than 250 words.

Can Deciding on a Career Path Early Lead to a More Satisfying Life?

It is true that some people know from an early age what career they want to pursue, and they are happy to spend the rest of their lives in the same profession. While I admit that this may suit many people, I believe that others enjoy changing careers or seeking job satisfaction in different ways.

On the one hand, having a defined career path can certainly lead to a satisfying working life. _____

_____

_____

_____

Unit 2　Job-Hopping

Viewing

The Secret to Being a Successful Freelancer

About the video clip

This video clip discusses the tips on becoming a successful freelancer.

Understanding the video clip

Filling in the blanks

Watch the video clip twice and fill in the blanks with what you hear.

Four tips by the speaker	Details
What you do.	When it comes to your offer, you have to be able to answer the following question: why would anyone _____?
Who _____.	After you determine what sets you apart, position yourself _____. In order for this to be effective, you must narrow your focus.
When it's time _____, understand the real value that you create.	You're not just being compensated for the time that _____. Ask yourself questions like: how does your service _____?
Make sure your price includes your taxes, your _____ and your _____.	When you're a freelancer, you are your own business.

True or false

Now watch the video clip again and decide whether the statements are true or false. Write "T" for "true" and "F" for "false".

1. Freelancers and artists are too often underpaid. ☐

2. In order to be effective, you must widen your focus. ☐

3. The freelancers are being compensated for everything they've learned and done over the years that make them excellent at what they do. ☐

4. If a potential customer balks at your pricing, you should apologize immediately. ☐

5. Focusing on making more money, rather than corrupting your creativity, can actually improve it by giving you more freedom of choice. ☐

Banked Cloze

There is a passage with ten blanks. You are required to select one word for each blank from the list of choices given in a word bank following the passage. Read the passage carefully before making your choices. Each choice in the bank is identified by a letter. Please write the corresponding letter for each item in the blanks. You may not use any of the words in the bank more than once.

The Ultimate Job-Hopper's Survival Guide[1]

NW: 220   GL: 7.2   AWL percentage: 8.64%   Keywords: job-hopper; resume; honesty

Candidates who changed jobs four or more times in 10 years are most likely to be labeled 1._____, according to a 2014 survey of 160 CFOs[2] by recruiting firm Robert Half International[3]. And 93% of hiring managers say they would 2._____ a candidate for taking on too many short job stints, according to findings.

"You need to be able to 3. _____ why that occurred and what you have learned," said David Jones, a Sydney-based managing director at Robert Half. And it's more important to vet the subsequent role to make sure it's a good fit. "You can't make one 4. _____and move

---

1   From BBC website.

2   CFO: Chief Financial Officer 首席财务官

3   Robert Half International: 罗致恒富。成立于 1948 年，总部位于美国加利福尼亚州，目前是会计、财务和科技领域招聘正式员工、固定期限员工和项目人员的专业招聘公司。

into another," he said.

Attitudes 5._____ by country, say hiring managers. For example, leaving a job in less than a year in Japan is still considered 6._____. Yet in expat-filled Singapore, and even China, job-hopping is 7. _____ becoming the norm, said Jones, whose team focuses on the Asia-Pacific region. Countries including the US and areas of Europe are more 8. _____ when it comes to hiring candidates with short stints on their CVs, added Butler.

No matter what your reason for leaving a job, 9. _____ is the best policy when it comes to your resume, particularly as social media and sites such as LinkedIn now make it easier for recruiters to do a(n) 10. _____ check and uncover previous experience.

A) vary	B) job-hoppers	C) honesty
D) appearance	E) taboo	F) explain
G) overlook	H) survey	I) dishonesty
J) teaching	K) mistake	L) increasingly
M) liberal	N) tobacco	O) background

OF JOB-HOPPING

Long Passage

You are going to read a passage with ten statements attached to it. Each statement contains information given in one of the paragraphs. Identify the paragraph from which the information is derived. You may choose a paragraph more than once. Each paragraph is marked with a letter. Please answer the questions by writing the corresponding letter after the statements.

The Pros and Cons of Job-Hopping[4]

NW: 1,039 GL: 10.1 **AWL percentage:** 7.6% **Keywords:** job hopping; pros; cons

A   Until recently, job-hopping was considered career suicide. Hiring managers were wary of resumes loaded with several short job stints; they'd think you were an unstable or disloyal employee. But things have changed. As job longevity becomes a thing of the past, employers and recruiters are beginning to have a different outlook on job-hopping.

B   According to the Bureau of Labor Statistics[5], the average number of years that US workers have been with their current employer is 4.6. Tenure of young employees (ages 20 to 34) is only half that (2.3 years).

---

4 From Forbes website.
5 Bureau of Labor Statistics: 美国劳工统计局。美国政府的一个机构，负责收集美国的就业率、工人薪酬、工作条件和物价等方面的数据。

C   Ryan Kahn, a career coach, founder of The Hired Group, star of MTV's *Hired*, and author of *Hired! The Guide for the Recent Grad*, agrees. He says the perception of job-hopping has changed over the past few years, "now becoming common to many." In the past this would have been something that would deter employers—but because of its frequency today, "job-hopping is replacing the concept of climbing the corporate ladder," he says.

D   So what exactly is job-hopping, and why do people do it?

E   Frank Dadah, a principal account manager and general manager at WinterWyman, says job-hopping is moving from one company to the next for either a lateral move or promotion. "It is usually considered job-hopping when you move from one company to the next every one to two years, have done it multiple times, and the reason for each move is due to something other than a layoff or company closing."

F   As it turns out, job-hopping can be extremely advantageous for certain types of people—if they do it for the right reasons, says Laurie Lopez, a partner and senior general manager in the IT Contracts division at WinterWyman. "For those in technology, for example, it allows them the opportunity to gain valuable technical knowledge in different environments and cultures. This can be more common for those specializing in development, mobile and Project Management. While job-hopping has a negative connotation; this is more about a resource providing value to a company, and then realizing there is nothing more to learn in that environment. In order to keep their skills fresh, it is necessary for technologists to remain current in a highly competitive market. Job-hopping is more common with employees that are less tenured, and feel confident in their skills to be able to move on without burning a bridge and can add value immediately in a new opportunity. With employers being more open to hiring job-hoppers, we expect the trend to continue."

G   The experts weighed in on the pros and cons of job-hopping.

H   Pros: Diverse background. Job-hoppers probably can point to experience in a number of different industries and different-sized companies, and exposure to a variety of challenges. Someone who has a diverse background is often more attractive to a potential employer because he/she potentially brings new ideas and ways of doing things.

I   Access to more information and resources. In most cases, the environment necessary to foster this growth can't be found under a single roof. Working in several different environments provides access to different resources—both human and informational—that one couldn't gain through a single employer.

J Exposure to different businesses and people. Job-hopping gives employees the opportunity to expand their experiences and shop around their talents. By working at multiple companies you will get to see ways that others are conducting business, while expanding your network to a whole new pool of professionals.

K A chance to find the right fit. Job-hopping gives you more opportunities to figure out what you like and don't, and what is important to you in a position and company. That way, when you are finally ready to settle down for several years, you know what you are looking for.

L Exposure to different jobs. Job-hopping gives an employee the opportunity to see what other jobs are out there. This could lead to an upgrade of title, salary, benefits or even work environment.

M Cons: Employers will be hesitant to invest in you. When jumping from job to job, you are showing future employers that there is a high likelihood that you will do the same to them. Also at most companies, putting in years of work with them proves your loyalty, helping to strengthen your job security. Loyalty goes a long way and from the employers perspective gives them dependability that they can count on.

N Your job may be less secure. If your employer is forced to lay off employees, you might be the first to go (given your track record of leaving companies quickly).

O Lack of satisfaction. Like the professional version of parenthood, one of the greatest satisfactions in a career is to be a part of a product's (or services) genesis and ultimate release. Where most products and services have a relatively long life-cycle, a job-hopper will never experience such satisfaction.

P They may question your judgment. The employer might wonder if you're prone to making bad decisions. One or two short stints might be acceptable if you went to a company that went bankrupt or were caught up in a layoff or just plain chose the wrong fit—but many of these might indicate you are someone who doesn't have good judgment.

Q They'll fear you'll leave at the first sign of trouble. The employer will wonder if you jump ship at the first sign of trouble, or if you always think the grass is greener someplace else.

R Lesson learned: There are many benefits and drawbacks of job-hopping—but if you do it for the right reasons and maintain healthy relationships with past employers, the pros should outweigh the cons and you'll be seen as a flexible, resourceful candidate.

"The most important thing is to be able to demonstrate that no matter where you worked or for how long, that you were someone who was critical to the success of a project or the company as a whole," says Steve Kasmouski, president of the Search Divisions at WinterWyman. "Your resume should tell the reader why you were important to the success of a project or company and should show that you have grown over time gaining increased responsibility, scope and success."

1. One was likely to be regarded as an unstable or disloyal employee if one's resume was loaded with several short job stints. ☐

2. Changing jobs can be immensely helpful for certain people, if they do so for the right purposes. ☐

3. Working in different companies can help you see how others are conducting business and expand your network to a whole new group of professionals. ☐

4. Having a lot of brief work experience might mean that you don't have sound judgment. ☐

5. An individual with varied experiences tends to be more desirable to a prospective employer because he/she is more likely to bring new concepts and approaches to the job. ☐

6. When the company is pressured to make layoffs, the frequent job-hopper will probably be the first to leave. ☐

7. One employee usually couldn't gain the access to different human and informational resources from a single employer. ☐

8. Job-hopping is moving from one company to another for either a lateral move or promotion. ☐

9. Your resume should explain why you were critical to the success of a project or company, and demonstrate how you have accumulated responsibility, depth, and success over time. ☐

10. Ryan Kahn believes that the public's view of job-hopping has shifted in recent years, and job-hopping is now popular to many. ☐

Short Passages

There are two passages in this part. Each passage is followed by some questions or unfinished statements. For each passage there are four choices marked A, B, C, and D. You should decide on the best choice and mark the corresponding letter.

Passage one

Why Young People in Britain Aren't Moving Job[6]

NW: 345 GL: 11.2 AWL percentage: 11.14%
Keywords: young people; moving job; unemployment

Older people tend to regard 20-somethings as typical types who <u>flit</u> from job to job. The reality is very different. Job mobility among the young has declined over the past decade.

Younger workers remain more wedded to their current jobs than they were before the recession. There is a similar trend in other rich countries, but it is particularly pronounced in Britain. According to Neil Carberry, chief executive of the Recruitment and Employment Confederation[7], a recruiters' trade body, the commonest complaint among his members is

---

6 From The Economist website.
7 Recruitment and Employment Confederation: 英国招聘和就业联合会

of a shortage of candidates.

This is a problem not just for employers, but also for employees. In the labour market, loyalty does not pay: shifting jobs tends to be a good way of getting a salary boost. In 2017, the average pay rise for a worker staying with the same employer was just 1.1% after inflation compared to 5.4% for someone making a change.

Researchers have long argued that having simple bad luck in entering the labour market during difficult times can have a lasting impact on young workers. Much of that research has focused on the so-called labour market scarring effect, by which those who experience unemployment early in their careers tend both to earn less than those who do not and to be at greater risk of future unemployment. Young people who experienced unemployment after the early 1980s or early 1990s recessions felt these effects for around ten years. Regional variations in housing costs may also play a role, <u>dampening down on</u> long-distance moves and hence overall labour market mobility.

These figures may help explain the puzzle of Britain's awful productivity, which is lower than the competitor's and growing only feebly. If workers do not move from job to job, resources will move more slowly from low-productivity firms to high-productivity ones.

On many measures Britain's labour market looks in rude health. But until 20-somethings start, once again, moving jobs and pushing for higher wages, it may not feel that way to many young people. Britain could do with its millennials acting a little more entitled.

1. What does the underlined word "flit" (Line 1, Para. 1) mean?

    A. Remain.

    B. Change.

    C. Fly.

    D. Choose.

2. Which statement is NOT true according to the second paragraph?

    A. Younger employees are more committed to their current jobs than they were prior to the recession.

    B. Growing faithfulness to jobs can be seen in many wealthy nations.

    C. This trend to stay with the current job is especially prominent in Britain.

    D. A shortage of professionals becomes the most frequent concern among members of a recruiters' trade body.

3. According to Paragraph 3, which one does NOT support the argument that "In the labour market, loyalty does not pay"?

   A. This is a problem both for employers and employees.

   B. Changing jobs is a common way to increase one's pay.

   C. In 2017, the average pay rise for a worker staying with the same employer was just 1.1%.

   D. In 2017, the average pay rise for someone making a job change was 5.4%.

4. Which statement is true about "labour market scarring effect"?

   A. Entering the labour market during difficult times can have a lasting impact on young workers.

   B. Those who experience unemployment early in their careers tend to earn more than those who do not.

   C. Those who experience unemployment early in their careers tend to be at lower risk of future unemployment.

   D. Young people who experienced unemployment after the early 1980s or early 1990s recessions felt these effects for around five years.

5. What does the underlined phrase "dampening down on" (Line 7, Para. 4) mean?

   A. Wetting.

   B. Humidifying.

   C. Reducing.

   D. Controlling.

Youngsters' Job Preferences and Prospects Are Mismatched[8]

NW: 373   GL: 10.0   AWL percentage: 9.73%   Keywords: youngster; job; mismatch

The world of work is changing. Are people ready for the new job outlook? A survey of 15-year-olds across 41countries by the OECD[9], a club of mostly rich countries, found that teenagers may have unrealistic expectations about the kind of work that will be available.

Four of the five most popular choices were traditional professional roles: doctors, teachers, business managers and lawyers. Teenagers underlined clustered around the most popular jobs, with the top ten being chosen by 47% of boys and 53% of girls. Those shares were significantly higher than when the survey was conducted back in 2000.

The rationale for this selection was partly down to wishful thinking on the part of those surveyed (designers, actors and musical performers were three of the top 15 jobs). Youth must be allowed a bit of hope.

Furthermore, teenagers can hardly be expected to have an in-depth knowledge of the minutiae of labour-market trends. They will definitely encounter doctors and teachers in their daily lives. Other popular professions, such as lawyers and police officers, will be familiar from films and social media. But many people end up in jobs they would not have heard of in their school years. You settle for what is available.

Some parts of the OECD survey are disturbing. Even though top performers in maths or science are evenly matched among males and females, a gender gap persists in terms of aspiration. More boys than girls expect to work in science or engineering—the average gap across the OECD is more than ten percentage points. The problem continues in higher education; with the exception of biological and biomedical sciences, degrees in stem subjects (science, technology, engineering and maths) are male-dominated. In America, women earn just 35.5% of undergraduate stem degrees and 33.7% of PhDs.

The biggest problem in the labour market, then, may not be that teenagers are focusing on a few well-known jobs. It could be a mismatch: not enough talented women move into technology and not enough men take jobs in social care. Any economist will

---

8   From The Economist website.
9   OEDC: 经济合作与发展组织（Organization for Economic Co-operation and Development）。成立于 1961 年，简称经合组织，是由 36 个市场经济国家组成的政府间国际经济组织。

recognize this as an inefficient use of resources. Wherever the root of the problem lies—be it the education system, government policy or corporate recruiting practices—it needs to be identified and fixed.

1. **What does the underlined word "clustered" (Line 2, Para. 2) mean?**

    A. Scattered.

    B. Gathered.

    C. Worked.

    D. Engaged.

2. **What does the underlined word "those" (Line 2, Para. 3) refer to?**

    A. Professions.

    B. Adults.

    C. Teenagers.

    D. Interviewees.

3. **Which statement is NOT true according to Paragraph 4?**

    A. Teenagers tend to have an inadequate knowledge of the details of labour-market trends.

    B. Teenagers are bound to meet physicians and teachers in their daily lives.

    C. Teenagers can get familiar with other popular professions, like lawyers and police officers from films and social media.

    D. Many people find jobs they would have heard of when they were students.

4. **Some parts of the OECD survey are disturbing EXCEPT that _____.**

    A. top performers in maths or science are evenly matched among males and females

    B. boys are more likely than girls to want to work in science or engineering

    C. degrees in science, technology, engineering and maths are male-dominated

    D. American women earn just 35.5% of undergraduate stem degrees

10. **What is the author's attitude towards the mismatch in labour market?**

    A. Indifferent.

    B. Pessimistic.

    C. Optimistic.

    D. Concerned.

Reading Skills

Understanding Paragraphs I

English is a topic-centered language: a paragraph, or longer text, has a single main topic, and all the details relate to that topic. Writers in English almost always mention the topic at or near the beginning of a passage. Good readers look for the topic when they read. Here are some notes helping you to understand paragraphs:

1. Topic sentences

A paragraphs in English usually contains a topic sentence that lets the reader know what the paragraph is about. Although this sentence is usually near the beginning of the paragraph, it can also be found in the middle or at the end.

2. Topic sentences and main idea

In addition to stating the topic, most topic sentences also tell the writer's main idea, or in other words, the idea that the writer wants to express about the topic. To explain the idea, the writer includes several supporting details in the paragraph and these details are more specific than the main idea.

3. Inferring the main idea

In some paragraphs, the topic sentence may not state the complete main idea. The topic may be stated in one sentence, and the writer's idea about the topic may be expressed in another sentence or in several sentences in the paragraph. In this case, the reader must combine ideas from several sentences to infer the complete main idea.

4. Connecting ideas in paragraphs

Understanding a paragraph—or a longer passage—often involves more than just identifying the topic and main idea. It is also necessary to understand the way writers in English guide the reader through the logic of their ideas or show the connections between ideas.

Exercises

Please read the above reading skills of understanding paragraphs and use the means to finish the following exercises.

A. Until recently, job-hopping was considered career suicide. Hiring managers were wary of resumes loaded with several short job stints; they'd think you were an unstable or disloyal employee. But things have changed. As job longevity becomes a thing of the past, employers and recruiters are beginning to have a different outlook on job-hopping. (Long Passage: Paragraph 1)

1. The topic of this paragraph is _____.

2. The main idea of this paragraph is _____.

3. Hiring managers' attitude of job-hopping used to be _____, but now they _____.

B. Younger workers remain more wedded to their current jobs than they were before the recession. There is a similar trend in other rich countries, but it is particularly pronounced in Britain. According to Neil Carberry, chief executive of the Recruitment and Employment Confederation, a recruiters' trade body, the commonest complaint among his members is of a shortage of candidates. (Short Passage One: Paragraph 2)

4. The topic sentence of this paragraph is _____.

5. How does the author support the idea of the topic sentence in this paragraph?
_____.

C. Furthermore, teenagers can hardly be expected to have an in-depth knowledge of the minutiae of labour-market trends. They will have encountered doctors and teachers in their daily lives. Other popular professions, such as lawyers and police officers, will be familiar from films and social media. But many people end up in jobs they would not have heard of in their school years. You settle for what is available. (Short Passage Two: Paragraph 4)

6. The topic sentence of this paragraph is _____.

THINK

Academic Words in Use

Fill in the blanks in the following sentences with the appropriate words provided in the box below. Change the form of the words if necessary.

recruit	resume	longevity	professional	mismatch
identify	unemployment	dampen	recession	boost

1. Even young boys are now being _____ into the army.

2. Nothing you can say will _____ her enthusiasm.

3. She sent her _____ to 50 companies, but didn't even get an interview.

4. _____ has fallen/risen again for the third consecutive month.

5. There is a(n) _____ between the capacity of the airport and the large number of people wanting to fly from it.

6. The _____ has led to many small businesses going bankrupt.

7. You need to _____ your priorities.

8. She always looks very _____ in her smart suits.

9. The successful branding and marketing of the new beer has already _____ sales and increased profits.

10. Very few people have a career of great _____, constancy and consistency in films.

Writing

For this part, you are allowed 30 minutes to read the following paragraph and continue writing to make it a well-structured article. You should write at least 180 words but no more than 250 words.

Factors You Should Consider while Changing Your Job

Switching a job is not an easy task. One has to think about a number of aspects in order to reach any particular conclusion. Avoid taking any decision in a hurry because once you quit a job, the action is irreversible. There are important factors that you need to consider before making this career move.

_____

_____

_____

_____

_____

Unit 3 Financial Management

Viewing

How to Manage Your Student Loans

About the video clip

This video clip introduces several options available to the students who have a federal student loan.

Understanding the video clip

Fill in the second column with the answers that match the conditions in the first column.

Problems that you may encounter	Possible solutions
1. If you're having trouble making your loan payments,	
2. If you qualify,	
3. If you meet certain requirements,	
4. If you do not qualify for a deferment,	
5. If you have multiple federal loans,	

Further thoughts

Nowadays, some college students from poverty-stricken families apply for student loans in order to complete their college education. This phenomenon has triggered a continuous wave of discussion over its benefits and drawbacks. Could you please list some of them in the table below?

Benefits of student loans	Drawbacks of student loans
1.	1.
2.	2.
...	...

Banked Cloze

There is a passage with ten blanks. You are required to select one word for each blank from the list of choices given in a word bank following the passage. Read the passage carefully before making your choices. Each choice in the bank is identified by a letter. Please write the corresponding letter for each item in the blanks. You may not use any of the words in the bank more than once.

Money Management for College Students[1]

NW:375   GL:11.9   AWL percentage:6.53%
Keywords:money management; college student; savings plan

College is an experience that allows us to explore, try new things, and make our own decisions on a larger scale. It's a great time in our lives, but it can also be a very expensive 1._____. Positive financial decisions and personal accounting will help to make your life after college more 2._____. By planning ahead and starting to save early, students can set themselves up for success financially and 3._____.

Saving and budgeting for college can help to 4._____ stress once college application time rolls around, and there are many different options that students and their families can take 5._____ of. Personal savings plans are always available, as are other savings options.

---

1 From IGNITESPOT website.

Self-discipline in saving and accurate bookkeeping are crucial when saving for college, as that first experience out of one's 6._____ home and the new freedom to make decisions for one's self-regarding money and spending come with many new temptations. Late nights out with friends, personal expenses, and maybe a need for the latest computer and electronics for that new dorm room can really add up and subtract from your rainy-day funds and money meant for one's 7._____. Stay focused and manage your money with long-term goals in mind: if what you're looking to buy won't help you reach those goals, you might be better off putting that money into savings.

Budgeting for your living expenses and monthly bills is a great first step in creating the savings plan you'll need to 8._____. Make a list of the bills you pay every month, then add in an estimated amount spent on personal items and groceries. Subtract that from your monthly income, and the amount you have left over is the amount that could be 9._____ into savings. That amount could also be used to pay some of the principal of any existing student loans while you're still attending school. This is a great option for students, as it allows them to 10._____ their student loan debt even before the interest kicks in and payments begin. Remember that most student loans do not need to be repaid while one is enrolled in school, so any dent that a student can put into their overall debt will help minimize their repayment amounts upon graduation.

A) alleviate	B) manageable	C) education
D) succeed	E) childhood	F) guide
G) advantage	H) contributes	I) academically
J) relating	K) investment	L) deposited
M) practically	N) minimize	O) provide

Long Passage

You are going to read a passage with ten statements attached to it. Each statement contains information given in one of the paragraphs. Identify the paragraph from which the information is derived. You may choose a paragraph more than once. Each paragraph is marked with a letter. Please answer the questions by writing the corresponding letter after the statements.

10 Money Management Tips for College Students[2]

NW: 1,096 GL: 7.3 AWL percentage: 4.29% Keywords: college student; loan; manage

A　　Unless you recently won the lottery, managing your money is likely a priority for you. Money management can feel monstrous and overwhelming, and when you're a student, balancing that bank account might seem doubly difficult.

B　　Going back to school may have prompted you to quit your second job in order to balance your new load of homework plus your other life responsibilities. Or maybe you've just seen the bill for your textbooks this semester and felt your stomach drop. Or it's possible you've just never really had to pay much attention to how much you spent on groceries or where that monthly Spotify subscription left your checking account.

2　From RASMUSSEN UNIVERSITY website.

C Whatever the culprit is, you know you need some help with managing money in college and we're here to help. We gathered tips from both financial experts and college students like you. Take a look at these 10 quick tips for mastering money management.

D **Budget for everything.** It can be easy to assume bills are the only thing you need to include in your monthly budget. Wrong! Those Starbucks coffee runs can add up fast. "The biggest thing I've learned is to have a budget for practically everything," says Yogin Patel, a sophomore at Arizona State University. "That means dedicate funds every month towards eating out, going to the movies, late-night snacks, books and supplies, socializing, etc. Keep in mind these budgets should let you save a portion of money every month, which is key." So where do you even start with creating a budget? Check out these basic budgeting apps!

E **Purchase used schoolbooks and sell your old ones.** Prices for certain textbooks have reached astronomical levels. It can also be difficult to get yourself over to the bookstore at the start of the semester when you know you're about to spend way more than you'd like. Search on Amazon for used textbooks, or shop places like Chegg[3], which hold loads of used textbooks for much less than if you bought them from your university bookstore. Another money-saving tactic would be to take advantage of any eBook offerings from your school.

F **Automate your savings.** It might feel fruitless to put away a bit of your paycheck into savings each month, but that kind of perseverance pays off in the long run. If you're one who struggles to save a portion of your earnings on pay day, make the decision once and for all and automate your savings. Most banks have a link on their websites in order to help you set this up. If you run into questions, call your bank teller and inquire about your options.

G **Get creative and find fun for free.** It's tempting to go out to eat and plan social activities that revolve around spending money. After all, what else is there to do in life that doesn't cost money? Well—a lot of things! David Bakke, a finance expert at Money Crashers[4], suggests replacing a few nights of barhopping with some at-home entertainment. Host a game night or rent a movie and enjoy a little entertainment free of charge. There's a good chance you can find a few friends who are on-board with saving some cash.

H **Steer clear of automated payments.** This is different from automating your savings. We live in an age where "lazy" shopping is becoming the new norm for many.

---

3 Chegg: 一家专门从事在线出租书籍的学术公司，总部位于美国加利福尼亚州圣克拉拉。该公司的业务主要针对高中生和大学生。

4 Money Crashers: 该网站致力于教育个人在信贷、债务、投资、教育、房地产、保险等方面做出明智的决定。

Automated payments for subscription services like Spotify[5] can add up quickly. Beware of media, fashion and other shopping subscriptions that require a monthly fee. Instead, allocate that money toward some necessities—or just save it altogether! While you might miss your monthly box of makeup samples while you're in school, bypassing those fees will take some of the sting out of paying tuition.

I **Cook at home.** Cooking at home doesn't mean you can never eat out. But if grabbing a salad from the local deli or swinging by the Dairy Queen after dinner has become a habit, try and cut back a bit. Cooking at home can be fun, inventive and even a great social activity. While it may require some planning ahead, a lot of money can be saved by purchasing ingredients from your local supermarket and making the most of leftovers.

J **Earn some extra cash.** "Work as much as you can without hindering your studies," says Chenell Tull from BrightCents.com. "Even a part-time job is great to give you some spending money and help pay off student loan interest while you are in school." Depending on what you're majoring in, freelance work may be a great option to make a little money on the side. If your degree doesn't offer many opportunities for freelance work, consider other creative ways to make money. Start an Etsy[6] shop, sell some clothes you've been meaning to get rid of or host a garage sale with your friends.

K **Pay in cash.** Swiping your credit card at the register is simple—sometimes a little too simple! It's easy to forget that equates to actual money. Once you get your paycheck and allocate what needs to go to tuition, bills and other monthly payments, use cash for other areas of your budget. Handing a crisp twenty-dollar bill to the grocery store clerk might feel different to you than paying with plastic, but it will help you avoid overspending. Once the cash is gone, it's gone!

L **Use online coupons.** Many businesses offer different deals online than they would if you were to purchase in-store. There are also plenty of online applications that can help alert you to promotional codes a website may offer. George Ruan helped create the browser extension Honey for just that purpose. "Using Honey can help college students save a lot of cash when they are shopping online and helps stretch a student budget," Ruan says. "It works on everything from pizza to textbooks!"

M **Beware of the "it's only 5 bucks!" syndrome.** "You can 5-buck your way to poverty and debt more quickly than you think," says Tana Gildea, author of *The Graduate's Guide to Money*. She explains that while a dollar a day spent in the vending machine may seem

---

5 Spotify: 一个正版流媒体音乐服务平台，2008 年 10 月在瑞典首都斯德哥尔摩正式上线。

6 Etsy: 一个网络商店平台，以手工艺成品买卖为主要特色。

harmless, it equates to $30 per month. "Did you really want to allocate $30 to soda, candy and crackers?" she asks. "Probably not, but it sneaks up on you. Try to reverse that trend and save a buck a day." Consider your purchases carefully, and include those extra snacks and smartphone app purchases in your budget. That way, you'll be sure to keep your finances in check.

1. To save money, you'd better stay at home for some entertainment instead of going to the bar. ☐

2. Used textbooks can be found in such shops as Chegg and Valore, and also Amazon. ☐

3. Using paper money will help you avoid overspending. ☐

4. At school you might pay little attention to the money spent on groceries or subscription of music. ☐

5. While shopping online, you can make use of the online coupons to save money. ☐

6. Cooking at home can not only save your money, but also bring you fun. ☐

7. You'd better avoid using media, fashion and other shopping subscriptions that require a monthly fee. ☐

8. It is necessary for you to budge almost every detailed expense in the campus. ☐

9. It's unwise to spend five bucks every day on soda, candy and crackers. ☐

10. It is advisable that you save a portion of your earnings every month and keep it for a long time. ☐

Short Passages

There are two passages in this part. Each passage is followed by some questions or unfinished statements. For each passage there are four choices marked A, B, C, and D. You should decide on the best choice and mark the corresponding letter.

Passage one

Is Student-Loan Forgiveness Unforgivable in Congress?[7]

NW: 425　GL: 16.6　**AWL percentage:** 5.82%　**Keywords:** student; debt; loan

Even before taking office, president-elect Joe Biden is already facing a political storm among his ideologically diverse base of supporters over the controversial issue of student-debt forgiveness.

Roughly 45 million Americans currently hold $1.6 trillion in student debt, with the average student-loan recipient owing between $20,000 and $25,000, according to the Federal Reserve[8]. Among those actively making payments on their debt, the average monthly installment is between $200 and $300. And with 5.3 million more people

---

7　From TIME website.
8　Federal Reserve: 美国联邦储备委员会

unemployed than in February, right before the US fell into a pandemic-induced recession, progressives say that student-debt forgiveness could be a boon for the economy.

"Student-debt cancellation feels like one of the most accessible executive actions to stimulate the economy at the moment," says Suzanne Kahn, director of the Education, Jobs and Worker Power program and the Great Democracy Initiative at the liberal Roosevelt Institute[9].

Kahn and others say the move would also help close the wealth gap between white Americans and people of color. Some 90% of Black students and 72% of Latino students take out loans for college vs. just 66% of white students, according to a 2016 analysis from the Consumer Financial Protection Bureau[10].

But the more moderate faction of Biden's base argues that sweeping student-loan forgiveness doesn't help the people who need aid most. Americans with college degrees, as a whole, have been less devastated by the economic effects of COVID-19 than their noncollege-educated counterparts. A September report from Pew Research Center found that only 12% of people with college degrees were having trouble paying bills as a result of the pandemic, compared with 34% of Americans with a high school diploma or less.

Others raise concerns about precedent if the government wipes out current student loans, future college students may have an incentive to take on debts, they argue, hoping they will also be forgiven. Colleges may in turn be inclined to raise their prices further.

In recent weeks, Biden has walked a fine line on the issue, offering support for a bill from House Democrats calling for $10,000 worth of student-loan forgiveness, but stopping short of endorsing anything close to a plan championed by Senators Elizabeth Warren and Chuck Schumer to issue $50,000 per borrower through executive action.

What's clear, according to experts on both sides of the aisle, is that economic crises worsen the problem of student debt. The last time the US dipped into a recession, state governments cut their investments in colleges and universities—which, in turn, raised their tuition prices and forced students to take on ever larger loans.

---

9 Roosevelt Institute: 罗斯福研究所（一个自由主义的美国智囊团）
10 Consumer Financial Protection Bureau: 美国消费者金融保护局

1. Before taking office, President Joe Biden was facing _____.

   A. an economic crisis

   B. a subprime lending crisis

   C. currency inflation

   D. an issue of student-debt cancellation

2. According to the Federal Reserve, what's the total sum of student debt among 45 million Americans?

   A. $20,000.

   B. $25,000.

   C. $1.6 trillion.

   D. $5.3 million.

3. Which of the following is NOT the possible result of the cancellation of student loan?

   A. It could help college students who need aid most.

   B. It could stimulate the economy at the moment.

   C. It would also help bridge the wealth gap between white Americans and people of color.

   D. It would make future college students have an incentive to take on debts.

4. Who has the most difficulty to pay the bill?

   A. People with college degrees.

   B. People with a high school diploma or less.

   C. People with master's degrees.

   D. People from Asian families.

5. What is the most direct consequence of the government's reduction of investment in universities?

   A. The decrease in the number of students.

   B. The rise of the tuition prices.

   C. The larger loans of poor students.

   D. The increase of the number of dropouts.

The Smartest Way to Spend Your Tax Refund[11]

NW: 443   GL: 10.0   **AWL percentage:** 5.04%
Keywords: tax refund; splurge; delayed gratification

In 2016, the average American received a tax refund of about $2,860, and the IRS[12] predicts similar numbers this year. There's no question about what a financial planner would tell you to do with such a sudden windfall: invest 90% of it toward paying down your debts, bolstering an emergency expense fund, and saving for retirement. This is all sound advice. But that still leaves 10%, or roughly $300, for selfish splurging, and we'd like to remind you that money actually can buy you happiness. Here, according to the latest research, are the four smartest ways to invest in joy:

Spend it on someone you love. This point may be the most important: people who spend money on others are measurably happier than people who spend on themselves. It feels really good to give, and if you give to someone extremely dear to your heart—say, your kid, partner, or parents—then your fleeting happiness takes on a new life as something else: meaning.

Give yourself something to look forward to. As we noted above, delayed gratification can be your friend, and thinking about something fun can be as rewarding as actually doing it. Let's say you used your splurge fund to book a weekend trip for three months from now. Not only do you get the enjoyment of experiencing the trip itself, but you also get three months of anticipatory planning. Thanks to a phenomenon that behavioral researchers call the "drool factor," delayed gratification gives you time to build up positive expectations, increasing your overall enjoyment.

Buy experiences, not stuff. There's an inherent thrill to shopping, but for most purchases the emotional high tends to ware off pretty quickly. One case where this is not true: buying experiences—out of town trips, concert tickets, spa days, notches on your bucket list and so on. The same way investing in a savings account compounds your earnings over time, study after study shows that investing in an experience compounds your happiness upon future reflection.

Recognize it as a treat. Tax refunds, like birthdays and polite relatives, come but once a

---

11 From Reader's digest website.
12 IRS: Internal Revenue Service 美国国家税务局，隶属于财政部。

year. If you use some of your money to buy something that you wouldn't normally <u>splurge</u> on, it will bring you more enjoyment than a routine purchase. On a cognitive level, it's sort of like the difference between watching your favorite TV show live as it airs week-by-week versus binge-watching every episode at once. Research shows that taking breaks between episodes notably increases the enjoyment of watching the show. In other words, there can be too much of a good thing—so don't splurge on something you could buy any day of the week.

1. **A financial planner would tell you to do the following EXCEPT_____ after receiving the tax refund.**

   A. paying down your debts

   B. bolstering an emergency expense fund

   C. buying luxury goods that you've been longing for

   D. saving for retirement

2. **What is the reason for your spending money on those who you love?**

   A. Because it feels really good to give.

   B. Because they are your family members.

   C. Because they once gave you help.

   D. Because they also bought things to you.

3. **Which of the following words is in closest meaning to the underlined word "splurge" (Line 2, Para. 5)?**

   A. Spend.

   B. Pay.

   C. Cost.

   D. Charge.

4. **What's the major difference between "buying material goods" and "buying experiences"?**

   A. An experiential purchase can make a buyer realize his value.

   B. An experiential purchase can make buyers happier than a material purchase.

   C. Investing in an experience will make a buyer think more about his future.

   D. An experiential purchase will save time.

5. **What does the writer mean by using the analogy of watching favorite TV shows once a week?**

   A. It brings you greater pleasure to watch an episode of your favorite TV show.

   B. A routine purchase will bring you more enjoyment.

   C. Taking breaks between episodes increases the enjoyment of watching the show.

   D. To buy something that you wouldn't buy every day will bring you more enjoyment.

Reading Skills

Understanding Paragraphs II

Comprehending what you're reading involves having a system of reading strategies that you can easily tap into. Effective readers will employ several of these strategies to rapidly understand what they're reading:

1. Identifying the topic of a paragraph

The topic is the word or phrase that best describes what all of the sentences in the paragraph are about. Words relating to the topic are usually repeated several times in a paragraph. Looking for these words can help you focus on the topic.

2. Identifying the topic sentences

The topic sentence is the most important sentence in a passage. Carefully worded and restricted, it helps keep a passage consistent and coherent. An effective topic sentence also helps readers grasp the main idea quickly. As you read, pay close attention to the topic sentences.

Exercises

Please read the Long Passage again and identify the topic sentence of each paragraph from Paragraph D to Paragraph H.

Paragraph D: _____

Paragraph E: _____

Paragraph F: _____

Paragraph G: _____

Paragraph H: _____

THINK

Academic Words in Use

Fill in the blanks in the following sentences with the appropriate words provided in the box below. Change the form of the words if necessary.

cancel	access	recognize	maintain	devastation
commerce	overwhelm	behavior	automate	initiate

1. The legal aid system should be _____ to more people.

2. It is the _____ responses which allow man to live in a cold climate.

3. Other than blowing up a tire I hadn't done any car _____.

4. The town has changed beyond _____ since I was last here.

5. Each company is fighting to protect its own _____ interests.

6. The official explanation for the _____ of the party conference is that there are no premises available.

7. The equipment was made on highly _____ production lines.

8. She knew she had to take the _____ and maintain an aggressive game throughout.

9. The _____ majority of those present were in favor of the plan.

10. Back on land, farmers are also suffering from the _____ drought.

Writing

For this part, you are allowed 30 minutes to read the following paragraphs and continue writing to make it a well-structured article. You should write at least 180 words but no more than 250 words.

Is the Wide Use of Private Cars More Destructive or Constructive?

Nowadays, the number of private cars is consistently on the rise. Obviously, a car owner is offered a more flexible schedule than those who rely on public transportation. Apart from that, being more mobile is considered as another big advantage. However, the prevalence of private cars has brought about many a problem that cannot be neglected.

First, the popularization of vehicles poses heavy threats to the environment.

_____

_____

_____

Unit 4 Why Do We Travel?

Viewing

The Point of Travel

About the video clip

This video clip discusses the reasons why people travel.

Understanding the video clip

Fill in the blanks with missing words that you hear from the video clip.

1. The point of travel, in brief, is to go to places that can help us in our _____ evolution.

2. Every location in the world contains qualities that can support some kind of _____ change inside a person.

3. Utah Desert in America is a place with perspective, free of _____ with the petty and the narrow-minded.

4. People in the Middle Ages would head out for a pilgrimage to _____with relics of a saint or a member of the holy family when there was something wrong with them.

5. Although modern people no longer believe in the divine power of journeys, certain parts of the world still have a power to change and mend the _____ parts of us.

6. People who are concerned with being admired and famous might be sent to _____ the ruins of Detroit.

7. We should become more _____ travelers on a well-articulated search for qualities that places possess, like calm or perspective, sensuality or rigor.

8. Traveling can be perceived as a way of helping us to grow into better _____ of ourselves.

Further thoughts

With the rapid development of Internet technology, more and more online business platforms have been developed. The prevalence of e-commerce has triggered a heated discussion over whether business travel is still necessary or not. What's your point of view?

Business travel is necessary	Business travel is unnecessary
1.	1.
2.	2.
…	…

Banked Cloze

There is a passage with ten blanks. You are required to select one word for each blank from the list of choices given in a word bank following the passage. Read the passage carefully before making your choices. Each choice in the bank is identified by a letter. Please write the corresponding letter for each item in the blanks. You may not use any of the words in the bank more than once.

Four Big Benefits of Business Travel[1]

NW: 326 GL: 12.4 AWL percentage: 7.16%
Keywords: benefit; business travel; communication

There are many ways corporate travel can benefit your business, from the obvious to the more subtle. Consider the facts:

Traveling is a great networking 1._____ for any company. Whether you are hoping to complete a business deal on a trip, need your employees to attend a training event, or just want to host an event in a different 2._____, there are networking opportunities when you land—and beforehand too. Many airlines have created lounges ideal for networking before you board, while hotels are beginning to build co-working lounge spaces for on-the-go travelers looking to build connections. If that's not enough, a survey by Virgin Atlantic[2]

---

1 From WorldTravelService website.
2 Virgin Atlantic: 维珍航空。是英国维珍大西洋航空公司 Virgin Atlantic Airways 的简称，于 1984 年成立，提供来往英国的洲际长途航空服务。

3._____ that one in five people have done business with someone they met on a plane.

Traveling can provide motivation and build company morale. Your employees will be happy to have the opportunity to travel and experience new cultures and places, leaving them engaged, motivated, and 4._____. Plus, corporate travel is an excellent opportunity for team building events that will bring your 5._____ together, so that they can work better with one another when they get back to the office.

Travel can foster creativity and 6._____. Traveling allows you to experience different cultures that can provide you with a new way of looking at things and because you never know what you'll have to deal with on the way, it can be a great way to learn 7._____ problem-solving. Virgin Atlantic even found that one in four of those surveyed found their best ideas while on a flight.

In-person meetings can be more effective in closing deals with more 8._____ partners, vendors, or customers. A study by UK company Concur found that 98 percent of businesses believe 9._____ contact is more effective in building relationships than meetings by phone or through email. If you work with companies that are further away, even 10._____, your business may benefit from the face-to-face communication that only traveling to meet them can afford.

A) productive	B) opportunity	C) inspiration
D) location	E) face-to-face	F) nature
G) achieve	H) estimates	I) employees
J) constructive	K) effective	L) international
M) lightening	N) distant	O) chiefly

Long Passage

You are going to read a passage with ten statements attached to it. Each statement contains information given in one of the paragraphs. Identify the paragraph from which the information is derived. You may choose a paragraph more than once. Each paragraph is marked with a letter. Please answer the questions by writing the corresponding letter after the statements.

Why We Travel[3]

NW: 1,037   GL: 8.3   AWL percentage: 2.92%   Keywords: travel; cognition; pleasure

A   It's 4:15 in the morning and my alarm clock has just stolen away a lovely dream. My eyes are open but my pupils are still closed, so all I see is gauzy darkness. For a brief moment, I manage to convince myself that my wakefulness is a mistake, and that I can safely go back to sleep. But then I roll over and see my zippered suitcase. I let out a sleepy groan: I'm going to the airport.

B   The taxi is late. There should be an adjective to describe the state of mind that comes from waiting in the orange glare of a streetlight before drinking a cup of coffee. And then the taxi gets lost. And then I get nervous, because my flight leaves in an hour. And then we're here, and I'm hurtled into the harsh glow of Terminal B, running with a

---

3 From The Guardian website.

suitcase so I can wait in a long security line. My belt buckle sets off the metal detector, my 120ml stick of deodorant is confiscated, and my left sock has a gaping hole.

C   And then I get to the gate. By now you can probably guess the punchline of this very banal story: my flight has been cancelled. I will be stuck in this terminal for the next 218 minutes, my only consolation will be a cup of caffeine and a McGriddle[4] sandwich. And then I will miss my connecting flight and wait, in a different city, with the same menu, for another plane. And then, 14 hours later, I'll be there.

D   Why do we travel? It's not the flying I mind—I will always be awed by the physics that gets a fat metal bird into the upper troposphere. The rest of the journey, however, can feel like a tedious lesson in the ills of modernity, from the pre-dawn X-ray screening to the sad airport malls peddling valueless souvenirs. It's globalization in a nutshell, and it sucks.

E   And yet here we are, herded in ever greater numbers on to planes that stay the same size. Sometimes we travel because we have to. Because in this digital age there is still something important about the analogue handshake. Or eating Mum's turkey at Christmas.

F   But most travel isn't non-negotiable. (In 2008 only 30% of trips over 50 miles were made for business.) Instead, we travel because we want to, because the annoyances of the airport are outweighed by the thrill of being in someplace new. Because work is stressful and our blood pressure is too high and we need a vacation. Because home is boring. Because the flights were on sale. Because New York is New York.

G   Travel, in other words, is a basic human desire. We're a migratory species, even if our migrations are powered by jet fuel and Chicken McNuggets[5]. But here's my question: Is this collective urge to travel—to put some distance between ourselves and everything we know—still a worthwhile compulsion? Or is it like the taste for saturated fat—one of those instincts we should have left behind in the Pleistocene epoch[6]? Because if travel is just about fun, then I think the new security measures at airports have killed it.

H   The good news, at least for those of you reading this while stuck on a tarmac, is that pleasure is not the only consolation of travel. In fact, several new science papers suggest that getting away—and it doesn't even matter where you're going—is an essential habit of effective thinking. It's not about a holiday, or relaxation, or sipping daiquiris on an unspoilt tropical beach. It's about the tedious act itself, putting some miles between

---

4 McGriddle: 麦满分，欧美最佳麦当劳产品
5 Chicken McNuggets: 麦乐鸡块
6 the Pleistocene epoch: 更新世时期

home and wherever you happen to spend the night.

I   Let's begin with the most literal aspect of travel, which is that it's a verb of movement. Thanks to modern engine technology, we can now move through space at an inhuman speed. The average walker moves at 3mph, which is 200 times slower than the cruising speed of a Boeing 737. There's something inherently useful about such speedy movement, which allows us to switch our physical locations with surreal ease. For the first time in human history, we can outrun the sun and segue from one climate to another in a single day.

J   The reason such travels are mentally useful involves a quirk of cognition, in which problems that feel "close"—and the closeness can be physical, temporal or even emotional—get contemplated in a more concrete manner. As a result, when we think about things that are nearby, our thoughts are constricted, bound by a more limited set of associations. While this habit can be helpful—it allows us to focus on the facts at hand—it also inhibits our imagination. Consider a field of corn. When you're standing in the middle of the field, surrounded by the tall cellulose stalks and fraying husks, the air smelling faintly of fertilizer and popcorn, your mind is automatically drawn to thoughts that revolve around the primary meaning of corn, which is that it's a plant, a cereal, a staple of farming.

K   But now imagine that same field of corn from a different perspective. Instead of standing on a farm, you're now in the midst of a crowded city street, dense with taxis and pedestrians. (And yet, for some peculiar reason, you're still thinking about corn.) The plant will no longer just be a plant: instead, your vast neural network will pump out all sorts of associations. You'll think about glucose-fructose syrup, obesity and Michael Pollan, author of *In Defense of Food*; ethanol made from corn stalks, popcorn at the cinema and creamy polenta simmering on a wood stove. The noun is now a loom of remote connections.

L   What does this have to do with travel? When we escape from the place we spend most of our time, the mind is suddenly made aware of all those errant ideas we'd suppressed. We start thinking about obscure possibilities—corn can fuel cars—that never would have occurred to us if we'd stayed back on the farm. Furthermore, this more relaxed sort of cognition comes with practical advantages, especially when we're trying to solve difficult problems.

1. Travels are useful because it makes you feel a kind of "closeness", both physically and mentally. ☐

2. I felt rather awkward during the security check. ☐

3. As a matter of fact, I am always afraid of taking airplanes. ☐

4. If you're in the midst of a crowded city street, you'll have associations different from those in the corn field. ☐

5. I believe that airport security measures have killed the pleasure of travel. ☐

6. I woke up in the early morning because I had to go on a business trip. ☐

7. I had to wait in the airport for nearly four hours because of the cancellation of the flight. ☐

8. The modern engine technology has made it possible that people can experience different climates in a single day. ☐

9. Some scientific studies show that getting away is an essential habit of effective thinking. ☐

10. Apart from doing business, there are dozens of reasons for travelling. ☐

Short Passages

There are two passages in this part. Each passage is followed by some questions or unfinished statements. For each passage there are four choices marked A, B, C, and D. You should decide on the best choice and mark the corresponding letter.

Passage one

Frequent Business Trips Can Lead to Burnout[7]

NW: 464   GL: 12.2   AWL percentage: 7.81%   Keywords: business trip; burnout; flexible

Business travel, as exciting as it sounds, is often a source of stress that companies may not be aware of. NexTravel, a corporate travel booking platform, recently conducted a study on the impact business travel has on employee productivity. The results resonated with my experience.

Nearly one in three (31.9%) business travellers say they experience difficulty staying on top of their workload when travelling.

Nearly three in ten (28.7%) feel like they have to be available constantly (checking emails, available via phone, etc.) while travelling for work.

---

7   From Forbes website.

Over a quarter (25.3%) would be more productive if they had free time while travelling.

Nearly a quarter (23.8%) feel like they have to work more or work overtime to make up for lost time while travelling.

One in six (16%) would be more productive if they had more say in when/how they travelled.

By addressing these concerns, companies can mitigate loss in productivity and even retain top talent in the long run. Here are some steps they can take, according to Wen-Wen Lam, CEO and Founder of NexTravel.

Adapt more flexible business travel policies. One of the biggest changes employers can make is incorporating more flexibility and empowerment for employees to travel how they want. For example, one in five business travellers said they would be more productive if their company allowed bleisure travel, which gives them the power to decide if they want to have additional days for themselves. Moreover, one in three employees revealed wanting to be able to change their flight if they want to stay longer or leave earlier. Something as simple as allowing employees to fly on the day they want or have the option to extend their trip can be the best defense against burnout and a loss in productivity. Ultimately, one of the best ways to sustain productivity for employees on the road is to implement functional, high-performing technology that powers their work. One in five (20%) business travellers said they have been behind on work while travelling because of poor WiFi and connectivity issues.

Remember the concept of comfort is evolving for new generations. Companies need to think outside the box and realize what comfort actually means to modern travellers. Many people (one in three or 34.8%), for example, want options like Airbnb[8] instead of a hotel and would like weigh in on how the budget is spent. Furthermore, for companies that want to go the extra mile, 17.3% of business travellers identified a few specifics that would positively impact their experiences, like being able to bring their pet along (17.3%) or having extra items or activities paid for such as special city tours, airport lounge access, etc. If budget allows, these small acts of consideration go a long way in boosting productivity and maintaining employee happiness.

---

8 Airbnb: 全称 AirBed and Breakfast，中文名是"爱彼迎"。爱彼迎是一家联系旅游人士和家有空房出租的房主的服务型网站，它可以为用户提供多样的住宿信息。

1. **Which of the following statements about business trip is NOT true?**

   A. Business travel is not always as exciting as most people expect.

   B. One out of three business travellers find it hard to control their workload when travelling.

   C. More than half business travellers are busy checking emails and receiving phone calls while travelling for work.

   D. Nearly a quarter of business travellers have to work for extra hours to make up for lost time while travelling.

2. **The following statements about "bleisure travel" are true EXCEPT_____.**

   A. it is a misspelling of the word "leisure"

   B. it gives travelers the power to decide if they want to have additional days for themselves

   C. it reflects the flexibility of employers in empowering employees more freedom to travel

   D. "bleisure" is a word blended by "business" and "leisure"

3. **Which of the following elements may account for the low efficiency of employees on business trip?**

   A. Poor WiFi and connectivity issues.

   B. The tiring flight.

   C. The impact of jet lag.

   D. The constraints of the schedule.

4. **For new generations, "comfort" means the following EXCEPT_____.**

   A. to live in Airbnb instead of a hotel

   B. to make clear how the budget is spent

   C. to bring their pets along

   D. to have extra days for such as sightseeing in the target city

5. **What do you think is the author's attitude towards the steps in boosting productivity and maintaining employee happiness?**

   A. Neutral. B. Supportive. C. Distasteful. D. Objective.

The New Landscape of Business Travel[9]

NW: 454   GL: 11.6   AWL percentage: 7.10%
Keywords: business travel; landscape; generations

Like all forms of travel, business travel is constantly evolving. New trends arise, with new challenges. If you've been in the business travel landscape for a while, you've likely noticed how each generation of travellers and each new development in travel technology impacts your day-to-day life. Your future success in the landscape likely has depended upon your ability to adapt to these impacts.

If you're just now entering the business travel landscape, whether it be because of your first expedition into the professional world or just because you've switched jobs mid-career to something more travel-intensive, here's what you can expect.

Perk Versus Burden

More and more, business travel in any job is being seen as a perk, versus a burden. In previous decades, generations of businesspeople would begrudgingly travel off to a conference and not be able to wait until they got back home. They hated the thought of being on the road and tried to get out of business travel as much as possible.

New generations though, particularly millennials, take to business travel with zest. They see it as a perk and they're more than adept at staying productive while on the go. They're familiar with working remotely, love to see new places and like to travel overall, even if it does require them to attend a conference or spend most of their days in boardrooms.

In fact, these generations will actively seek out jobs that include business travel. Some admit they would change jobs in order to find one with more travel included.

For older generations, this can become a nuisance, as younger generations gain power and respect in the workplace because they're willing to take on all the business travel that their bosses could potentially request.

Bleisure Travel

Along these lines of generational differences, younger generations are starting to back

---

9 From Forbes website.

a trend called "bleisure travel." This just means that, to a business trip, a traveller might add three or four days of uninterrupted leisure time to further enjoy a destination and see it for themselves beyond the boardroom.

While companies might be slow getting behind this trend, as it takes travellers out of the office, it could prove to be a blessing. After all, a traveller extending their trip could actually lessen costs for the company, at least in terms of flights, assuming that the traveller pays for their extra hotel nights themselves.

Additionally, it's also seeming that business travellers who engage in bleisure travel are more likely to break up their vacation time over short periods of time, taking two or three days at once. This is versus leaving the office for one long stretch once a year, disengaging from the workplace for as much as two or three weeks.

1. **The following words can be used to describe business travel EXCEPT**
   _____.

   A. evolving

   B. developing

   C. boring

   D. challenging

2. **What does the underlined word "begrudgingly" (Line 2, Para. 3) mean?**

   A. Unwillingly.

   B. Hatefully.

   C. Readily.

   D. Quickly.

3. **Which of the following is NOT the characteristic of new-generation business travellers?**

   A. They often take business trips with enthusiasm.

   B. They hate jobs with frequent business travels.

   C. They love to see new places and work remotely.

   D. They take business trips as a special benefit.

4. According to the passage, why could travellers extending their trip lessen costs for the company?

    A. Because they will not take airplanes to travel.

    B. Because they will stay in guest houses instead of hotels.

    C. Because they will pay for their extra hotel nights themselves.

    D. Because they will work more diligently.

5. What does "This" in the last paragraph refer to?

    A. Bleisure travel.

    B. Taking a two-or-three-week holiday.

    C. Extending their trip.

    D. Taking a two-or-three-day holiday.

Reading Skills

Sequencing Information

When you sequence information, you put things in the order of their occurrence. This can help you understand how key events in a text relate to each other, such as cause and effect relationships. It is especially useful to sequence information from stories or biographical texts.

Exercises

Please read the first three paragraphs of the Long Passage "Why We Travel" and put the following sentences in the correct order by using the skill of sequencing information.

A. It's 4:15 in the morning and my alarm clock has just stolen away a lovely dream. My eyes are open but my pupils are still closed, so all I see is gauzy darkness. For a brief moment, I manage to convince myself that my wakefulness is a mistake, and that I can safely go back to sleep. But then I roll over and see my zippered suitcase. I let out a sleepy groan: I'm going to the airport.

B. The taxi is late. There should be an adjective to describe the state of mind that comes from waiting in the orange glare of a streetlight before drinking a cup of coffee. And then the taxi gets lost. And then I get nervous, because my flight leaves in an hour. And then we're here, and I'm hurtled into the harsh glow of Terminal B, running with a suitcase so I can wait in a long security line. My belt buckle sets off the metal detector, my 120ml stick of deodorant is confiscated, and my left sock has a gaping hole.

C. And then I get to the gate. By now you can probably guess the punchline of this very banal story: my flight has been cancelled. I will be stuck in this terminal for the next 218 minutes, my only consolation will be a cup of caffeine and a McGriddle sandwich. And then I will miss my connecting flight and wait, in a different city, with the same menu, for another plane. And then, 14 hours later, I'll be there.

1. The taxi gets lost.

2. I wake up at 4:15 in the morning.

3. I will be stuck in the terminal for the next 218 minutes.

4. I'm going to the airport by a taxi.

5. My flight has been cancelled.

6. I'm hurtled into the harsh glow of Terminal B.

THINK

Academic Words in Use

Fill in the blanks in the following sentences with the appropriate words provided in the box below. Change the form of the words if necessary.

imagine	contribute	power	vulnerable	compassion
anxious	flexible	isolate	potential	enthusiast

1. Her _____ about the world was amplifying her personal fears about her future.

2. They want jobs that provide security and _____, and they place relatively little importance on high pay.

3. This level of success would have been _____ just last year.

4. He appeared to be treating the _____ explosive situation with some sensitivity.

5. Many daughters assume that their mothers are _____.

6. The movement actively _____ women and gave them confidence in themselves.

7. These charities depend on the _____ feelings and generosity of the general public.

8. The winners were given a(n) _____ welcome when they arrived home.

9. The police said the attack was a(n) _____ incident.

10. These measures would make a valuable _____ towards reducing industrial accidents.

Writing

For this part, you are allowed 30 minutes to read the following paragraphs and continue writing to make it a well-structured article. You should write at least 180 words but no more than 250 words.

Is It Necessary to Travel Abroad to Learn about Foreign Countries?

Some people think that it is necessary to travel abroad to learn about other countries, but other people think that it is not necessary to travel abroad because all the information can be seen on TV and the Internet. I would argue that it is still of necessity to visit the nations to fully learn about them.

There is no denying that nowadays live videos and international television channels can provide first-hand information about the life in foreign countries.

_____

_____

_____

Unit **5** Being Friendly to the Environment

Viewing

Causes and Effects of Climate Change

About the video clip

This video clip discusses the causes and effects of climate change.

Understanding the video clip

Please fill in the blanks with proper words to match the causes of climate change in the left column with the effects in the right column.

Causes	Effects
1. pollution and overpopulation	_____
2. _____	increasing the earth's temperature
3. the burning of fossil fuels	_____
4. climate change	_____
5. _____	_____
6. exposure to higher levels of smog	_____

Further thoughts

   With the enhancement of people's awareness of environmental protection, more and more people advocate low-carbon life. As a college student, what do you think you can do to protect the environment?

Banked Cloze

There is a passage with ten blanks. You are required to select one word for each blank from the list of choices given in a word bank following the passage. Read the passage carefully before making your choices. Each choice in the bank is identified by a letter. Please write the corresponding letter for each item in the blanks. You may not use any of the words in the bank more than once.

Humanity Has Wiped out Many Animal Populations since 1970[1]

NW: 288   GL: 10.5   AWL percentage: 7.74%   Keywords: animal; extinction; humanity

"We are rapidly running out of time," said Prof Johan, a global sustainability expert. "Only by addressing both ecosystems and climate do we stand a chance of safeguarding a(n) 1._____ planet for humanity's future on Earth."

Many scientists believe the world has begun a sixth mass extinction. Other recent analyses have 2._____ that humankind has destroyed 83% of all mammals and half of plants since the dawn of civilization.

The Living Planet Index, produced by the Zoological Society of London, uses data on 16,704 populations of mammals, birds, fish, reptiles and amphibians, representing more

---

1 From The Guardian website.

than 4,000 species, to 3._____ the decline of wildlife. Between 1970 and 2014, the latest data 4._____, populations fell by an average of 60%. Four years ago, the decline was 52%. The "shocking truth", said Barrett, is that the wildlife crash is continuing.

"Wildlife and the ecosystems are vital to human life", said Prof Bob Watson, one of the world's most eminent environmental scientists, "and the 5._____ of nature is as dangerous as climate change". "Nature 6._____ to human wellbeing culturally and spiritually, as well as through the critical production of food, clean water, and energy, and through 7._____ the Earth's climate, pollution, pollination and floods," he said. "The Living Planet report clearly demonstrates that human activities are destroying nature at an unacceptable rate, 8._____ the wellbeing of current and future generations."

The biggest cause of wildlife losses is the destruction of natural 9._____, much of it to create farmland. Three-quarters of all land on Earth is now 10._____ affected by human activities. Killing for food is the next biggest cause—300 mammal species are being eaten into extinction—while the oceans are massively overfished, with more than half now being industrially fished.

A) track	B) available	C) destruction
D) revealed	E) respectively	F) current
G) significantly	H) attributes	I) threatening
J) habitats	K) stable	L) regulating
M) maintenance	N) contributes	O) vital

Long Passage

You are going to read a passage with ten statements attached to it. Each statement contains information given in one of the paragraphs. Identify the paragraph from which the information is derived. You may choose a paragraph more than once. Each paragraph is marked with a letter. Please answer the questions by writing the corresponding letter after the statements.

Do You Drink Bottled Water?[2]

NW: 845 GL: 14.4 **AWL percentage:** 8.28%
Keywords: bottled water; contamination; environmental crises

A   For years, the debate has raged on: Which is better, bottled water, or tap water?

B   Despite its ever-growing popularity in the US, bottled water is atrocious for the environment. To quote Harvard University's Office for Sustainability, "The entire life cycle of bottled water uses fossil fuels, contributes to global warming, and causes pollution."

C   Although water bottles are recyclable, Americans throw away about 80% of the bottles they use—and, by some estimates, Americans use 1,500 plastic bottles of water

---

2 From The Guardian website.

every second. Plastic bottles contribute immensely to global environmental crises, in part due to the fact that they disintegrate into microplastics, the presence of which are so ubiquitous that researchers recently discovered them in the placentas of unborn babies. Bottled water takes 2,000 times the energy to produce and ship than its tap equivalent. The extraction and manufacturing processes used by bottled water corporations can also have negative environmental and economic effects, and amount to the privatization and commodification of a limited and invaluable resource to which all should have a universal right.

D When clean, safe water is unavailable, drinking bottled water becomes a necessity. The average consumer, however, does not purchase bottled water out of need, but because it's convenient and often effectively marketed as purer or tastier than tap—despite the fact that it does not necessarily even come from the appealing sources consumers think it does. Bottled water is also about 3,000% more expensive per gallon than what's in the tap.

E When it comes to the health qualities of bottled water versus tap, differences are largely negligible. Both tap and bottled water are required to meet quality requirements set by the US Environmental Protection Agency[3](EPA) and Food and Drug Administration[4] (FDA) respectively. Contamination is always possible in either—and is an urgent issue affecting tap water in parts of the US—but by prevailing standards both are generally fine to drink.

F Prevailing standards, however, have not quite caught up to the threat of PFAS[5]—a group of industrial chemicals numbering in the thousands and used in a variety of consumer products. PFAS have been found in both tap and bottled water. There is currently no federal guidance on PFAS regulation, though there is evidence that the most-studied forms of PFAS are carcinogenic and linked to liver damage, thyroid disease, and pregnancy risks, among other adverse health effects.

G "PFAS have been found in the blood of over 98% Americans," Dr. Rebecca Aicher, project director at the Center for Scientific Evidence in Public Issues, told me. "Because the research has shown there may be human health effects, there's a lot of interest in where the exposure is coming from—and we know there is exposure from drinking water."

H According to the Environmental Working Group, as of January 2021, 2,337

---

3 US Environmental Protection Agency (EPA): 美国环境保护署
4 Food and Drug Administration (FDA): 美国食品和药物管理局
5 PFAS: 全氟烷基和多氟烷基物质的英文缩写形式，是耐高温且不易降解的化学合成物质，研究已经揭示它们对人类的健康和环境会造成负面影响。

locations in 49 states are known to have PFAS contamination in their water systems. Last autumn, Consumer Reports also found concerning levels of PFAS in popular bottled water brands, including Nestlé products from the Perrier and Poland Spring lines, and canned carbonated waters like Bubly and LaCroix, among others.

I So, where does this leave those of us who simply want to stay hydrated?

J "Most importantly," says Aicher, "municipal water must be tested to determine if there are PFAS in the water—that's the first step, to encourage states and communities to have sampling and monitoring plans for PFAS." Bottled water companies, it follows, must also be held accountable to test for PFAS.

K If there are PFAS in your drinking water, the wisest immediate option may be investing in a home water filter, and maintaining it responsibly, according to a 2020 study by researchers at Duke University and North Carolina State University. Scientists compared the level of contaminants remaining in water filtered through pitchers, in-fridge devices, under-sink reverse osmosis and two-stage filters, and whole-house systems.

L "All of the under-sink reverse osmosis and two-stage filters achieved near-complete removal of the PFAS chemicals we were testing for," Dr. Heather Stapleton, who worked on the study, said in a Duke University release. "In contrast, the effectiveness of activated-carbon filters used in many pitcher, countertop, refrigerator and faucet-mounted styles was inconsistent and unpredictable. The whole-house systems were also widely variable and in some cases actually increased PFAS levels in the water."

M Even then, there is the issue of what to do with your PFAS-riddled filter once you're finished with it. Effective water filters may remove PFAS, "but you're not actually destroying the PFAS. So once you've pulled the PFAS out of the water there's actually waste that needs to be dealt with, because the PFAS are still intact," says Aicher.

N If tossed into a landfill, PFAS will leech right back out into waterways. They can be incinerated at a very high temperature, but unless you have access to an industrial incinerator, you're stuck waiting for state intervention, or the EPA's action plan to address the presence of PFAS in drinking water to take meaningful effect in your community.

O As you can see, bottled water is atrocious for the environment. You're better off buying a water filter for healthier, tastier water.

1. Even though you've pulled the PFAS out of the water, there's still waste that needs to be dealt with. ☐

2. Bottled water is harmful to the environment because its life cycle uses fossil fuels, which are likely to cause pollution. ☐

3. Contamination is always possible in either tap water or bottled water. ☐

4. According to a study, the wisest way to eliminate PFAS in your drinking water is to buy a home water filter and maintaining it regularly. ☐

5. Many consumers buy bottled water just because it is convenient. ☐

6. The whole-house systems sometimes actually increased PFAS levels in the water. ☐

7. Researchers are trying to find out where the exposure of PFAS is coming from. ☐

8. Studies have found that PFAS are linked to some diseases and bring about adverse health effects. ☐

9. The government's intervention, or the EPA's action plan should assume the responsibility to address the presence of PFAS in drinking water. ☐

10. As plastic bottles can disintegrate into microplastics, it will cause global environmental crises. ☐

Short Passages

There are two passages in this part. Each passage is followed by some questions or unfinished statements. For each passage there are four choices marked A, B, C, and D. You should decide on the best choice and mark the corresponding letter.

Passage one

Aeroplanes and Global Warming[6]

NW: 450 **GL:** 12.2 **AWL percentage:** 4.51% **Keywords:** global warming; aeroplane; CO_2

For those lucky enough to have money to spend, and the free time to spend it in, there are a huge number of fascinating places to explore. The cost of air transport has decreased rapidly over the years, and for many people, especially in rich countries, it is now possible to fly around the world for little more than the contents of our weekly pay packets.

Unfortunately, planes produce far more carbon dioxide (CO_2) than any other form of public transport, and CO_2 is now known to be a greenhouse gas, a gas which traps the heat of the sun, causing the temperature of the Earth to rise. If global warming continues, we may also find that many tourist destinations such as the Maldives[7] will disappear under

---

6   From SME website.
7   Maldives: 马尔代夫群岛

water because of rising sea levels.

When you are waiting impatiently in a crowded departure lounge for a delayed flight or trying to find luggage which has gone astray, plane fares may seem unreasonably high, but in reality the damage caused by planes is not being paid for. Aircraft fuel is not taxed on international flights, and unlike cars, planes are not inspected for CO_2 emissions.

So what can be done to solve the problem? Well, although aircraft engine manufacturers are making more efficient engines and researching alternative fuels such as hydrogen, it will be decades before air travel is not damaging to the environment. Governments don't seem to be taking the problem seriously, so it is up to individual travelers to do what they can to help.

The most obvious way of dealing with the problem is to not travel by plane at all. Environmental groups like Friends of the Earth encourage people to travel by train and plan holidays nearer home. They also advise using teleconferencing for international business meetings, but most businesspeople still prefer to meet face-to-face.

However, there is a way of offsetting the carbon dioxide we produce when we travel by plane. A company called Future Forests, whose supporters include Coldplay[8] and Pink Floyd[9], offers a service which can relieve the guilty consciences of air travelers. The Future Forests website calculates the amount of CO_2 you are responsible for producing on your flight, and for a small fee will plant the number of trees which will absorb this CO_2. Another company, co2.org, offers a similar service, but invests your money in energy-saving projects such as providing efficient light bulbs to villagers in Mauritius[10].

Yesterday I returned to Japan from England and was happy to pay Future Forests 25 pounds to plant the three trees which balance my share of the CO_2 produced by my return flight. Now the only thing making me lose sleep is jet lag.

1. **According to the writer, what is the major reason for the popularity of the air transport?**

   A. People are becoming richer.

   B. The cost of air transport is descending.

   C. People have more free time.

   D. There are more and more airlines.

---

8 Coldplay: 酷玩乐队，英国摇滚乐队，1996 年成立于伦敦。

9 Pink Floyd: 平克·弗洛伊德，英国摇滚乐队，最初以迷幻与太空摇滚音乐赢得知名度，而后逐渐发展为前卫摇滚音乐。

10 Mauritius: 毛里求斯（非洲岛国）

2. **Which vehicle emits the most carbon dioxide?**

    A. Cars.

    B. Trains.

    C. Ships.

    D. Planes.

3. **Which of the following statements is NOT True?**

    A. If global warming continues, some areas of low latitudes will face the risk of being submerged by the rising sea level.

    B. Planes are not inspected for CO_2 emissions.

    C. The damage caused by planes is paid for by taxes levied on international flights.

    D. Aircraft engine manufacturers have been making more efficient engines to reduce CO_2 emission.

4. **The following are the suggested ways to deal with the problem by Friends of the Earth EXCEPT _____ .**

    A. never travel by plane any more

    B. to travel by train

    C. to use teleconferencing for international business meetings

    D. to choose a place close to home to spend holidays

5. **What's the writer's attitude towards the measure of paying a small fee to plant trees to offset the carbon dioxide?**

    A. Supportive.

    B. Opposed.

    C. Neutral.

    D. Ironic.

Harmony with Nature[11]

NW: 429   GL: 17.9   **AWL percentage:** 12.18%   **Keywords:** harmony; nature; sustainable

In 2009, the United Nations General Assembly proclaimed 22 April as International Mother Earth Day. In doing so, member states acknowledged that the Earth and its ecosystems are our common home, and expressed their conviction that it is necessary to promote harmony with nature in order to achieve a just balance among the economic, social and environmental needs of present and future generations. The same year, the General Assembly adopted its first resolution on Harmony with Nature.

The General Assembly has widely acknowledged that the world's depletion of natural resources and rapid environmental degradation are the result of unsustainable consumption and production patterns which have led to adverse consequences for both the Earth and the health and overall well-being of humanity. The scientific community has well-documented evidence that our present way of life, in particular our consumption and production patterns, has severely affected the Earth's carrying capacity.

Loss of biodiversity, desertification, climate change and the disruption of a number of natural cycles are among the costs of our disregard for nature and the integrity of its ecosystems and life-supporting processes. As recent scientific work suggests, a number of planetary boundaries are being transgressed and others are at risk being so in a business-as-usual world. Since the Industrial Revolution, nature has been treated as a commodity that exists largely for the benefit of people, and environmental problems have been considered as solvable through the use of technology. In order to meet the basic needs of a growing population within the limits of the Earth's finite resources, there is a need to devise a more sustainable model for production, consumption and the economy as a whole.

Devising a new world will require a new relationship with the Earth and with humankind's own existence. Since 2009, the aim of the General Assembly, in adopting its nine resolutions on Harmony with Nature, has been to define this newly found relationship based on a non-anthropocentric relationship with nature. The resolutions contain different perspectives regarding the construction of a new, non-anthropocentric paradigm in which the fundamental basis for right and wrong action concerning the environment is grounded not solely in human concerns. A step in this direction was further reaffirmed in the outcome document of the United Nations Conference on Sustainable Development (2012),

11 From Harmony with Nature (United Nations) website.

entitled "The future we want":

"We recognize that planet Earth and its ecosystems are our home, and that 'Mother Earth' is a common expression in a number of countries and regions, and we note that some countries recognize the rights of nature in the context of the promotion of sustainable development."

1. **Which of the following is NOT the reason why the United Nations General Assembly proclaimed 22 April as International Mother Earth Day?**

    A. The member states have acknowledged that the Earth and its ecosystems are our common home.

    B. The member states have realized the necessity to promote harmony with nature.

    C. It is of great significance to achieve a balance among the economic, social and environmental needs of present and future generations.

    D. This is a major decision reached by the permanent members of the United Nations.

2. **What is the deep root of the world's depletion of natural resources and rapid environmental degradation?**

    A. Overpopulation.

    B. Unsustainable consumption and production patterns.

    C. Deforestation.

    D. The emission of CO_2.

3. **The disregard for nature and the integrity of its ecosystems and life-supporting processes has caused the following problems EXCEPT _____.**

    A. desertification

    B. loss of biodiversity

    C. acid rain

    D. climate change

4. Which of the following statements is NOT true about the deeds of human beings to the nature?

   A. After the Industrial Revolution, human beings have done a lot to destroy the nature.

   B. Nature has been treated as a commodity that exists largely for the benefit of people.

   C. Environmental problems have been considered as solvable through the use of technology.

   D. Human beings have always been aware of the importance of keeping harmony with nature.

5. Which of the following do you think is NOT an action of sustainable development?

   A. Giving top priority to economic development.

   B. The construction of a new, non-anthropocentric paradigm.

   C. Rational utilization and optimal allocation of natural resources.

   D. Building a new relationship with the Earth and with humankind's own existence.

Reading Skills

Critical Reading: Determining the Purpose

With all the information that is available today, you must be on your guard as you read. Nothing is automatically true just because it is in print or on the Web. You need to develop the ability to read critically. That is, you need to ask questions like these about the text and about the writer:

- Where is this material from? Is this a valid source of information?

- Who is the writer? Is he or she qualified to write about this topic?

- Can I trust the information here?

- What is the writer's purpose in writing this?

- What is the writer's point of view about the topic?

- How does this information differ from what I already know?

The three main purposes for writing are:

- To inform—the author presents facts and explains ideas to the reader.

- To persuade—the author uses facts and opinions to argue for or against some ideas.

• To entertain—the author tries to amuse or interest the reader with humor, suspense, and stories.

A piece of writing can often fulfill more than one purpose. It can, in fact, be informative, persuasive, and entertaining all at once. However, the writer usually has one primary purpose in writing it.

How can you tell what the writer's purpose is?

• Look at the information in the passage. Does it contain a lot of facts? If it does, the purpose may be to inform or to persuade.

• Look at the language in the passage.

1) If it is neutral and objective, the purpose is probably simply to inform the reader.

2) If it includes terms that are strongly positive, negative, or emotional, the purpose is probably to persuade the reader.

3) If it includes situations or descriptions that are funny, surprising, or intriguing, the writer probably wants to entertain the reader.

Exercises

Read the following statements taken from the Long Passage and the Short Passages and determine the purpose of the writer: to inform, to persuade or to entertain.

1. Although water bottles are recyclable, Americans throw away about 80% of the bottles they use—and, by some estimates, Americans use 1,500 plastic bottles of water every second.

   _____

2. When it comes to the health qualities of bottled water versus tap, differences are largely negligible.

   _____

3. Bottled water is also about 3,000% more expensive per gallon than what's in the tap.

   _____

4. If there are PFAS in your drinking water, the wisest immediate option may be investing in a home water filter, and maintaining it responsibly.

   _____

5. As you can see, bottled water is atrocious for the environment. You're better off buying a water filter for healthier, tastier water.

_____

6. Governments don't seem to be taking the problem seriously, so it is up to individual travelers to do what they can to help.

_____

7. Now the only thing making me lose sleep is jet lag.

_____

8. The scientific community has well documented evidence that our present way of life, in particular our consumption and production patterns, has severely affected the Earth's carrying capacity.

_____

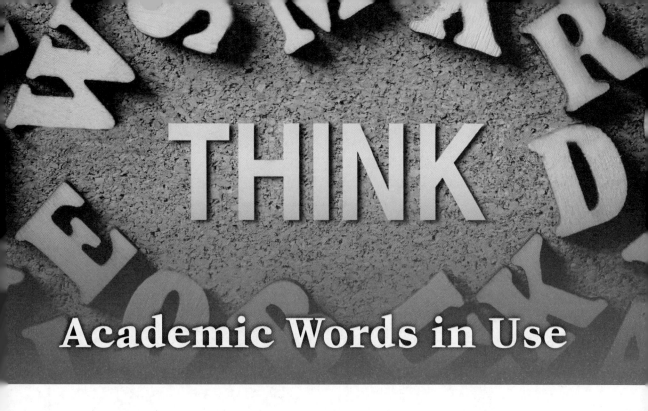

THINK

Academic Words in Use

Fill in the blanks in the following sentences with the appropriate words provided in the box below. Change the form of the words if necessary.

available	contaminate	consistent	consume	global
harmony	integrate	regard	resolve	sustain

1. Life on Earth will become _____ unless population growth is held in check.

2. We are doing our best with the limited resources _____.

3. If everyone can reach out a helping hand to others, the world around us will be more and more _____.

4. _____ rather than saving has become the central feature of contemporary societies.

5. To modernize China's higher education, we must think _____ and act locally.

6. Her actions manifested a complete _____ for personal safety.

7. The outburst was _____ with the image he has cultivated.

8. His music is a(n) _____ of tradition and new technology.

9. The packaging must provide an effective barrier to prevent _____ of the product.

10. The government is pressing for an early _____ of the dispute.

Writing

For this part, you are allowed 30 minutes to read the following paragraphs and continue writing to make it a well-structured article. You should write at least 180 words but no more than 250 words.

Should We Spend Our Time and Energy Protecting Wild Animals or Human Beings?

In these days, with some improper human activities such as hunting rare animals and the extinction of some endangered animals, there has been an intense debate about whether too many resources, including time and money, should be allocated to preserve wild animals.

Proponents of this opinion may argue that human beings could have done more to safeguard wild animals from being extinct, so that less animals would have died out or diminished.

Unit **6** Internet and Life

What Is Cloud Computing?

Viewing

What Is Cloud Computing?

About the video clip

This video clip discusses what Cloud computing[1] is and how it can influence our lives.

Understanding the video clip

Filling in the blanks

Watch the video clip twice and fill in the blanks.

1. What is Cloud computing?

Cloud computing is the on-demand _____, with pay-as-you-go[2] pricing.

2. What can the Cloud be used for?

Organizations of every type, size and industry are using the Cloud for a wide variety of use cases, such as data backup, _____, email,

---

1 Cloud computing: 云计算是分布式计算的一种，指的是通过网络"云"将巨大的数据计算处理程序分解成无数个小程序，然后，通过多部服务器组成的系统处理和分析这些小程序，得到结果并返回给用户。

2 pay-as-you-go: 指的是一种付费方式，当费用产生时才进行付费，而无需预先交钱，即：先使用后付费。

_____, software development and testing, _____, and customer facing web applications.

3. How will Cloud computing influence your business?

With Cloud computing your business can become _____, and deploy globally in minutes.

4. What can you do with the Cloud computing?

You can _____ in a matter of minutes and _____ several orders of magnitude faster than before.

This gives you the freedom to experiment and test new ideas to _____ and transform your business.

Matching

Now watch the video clip again, match the sentences and fill in the blanks.

- Health care companies are using the Cloud

- Financial services companies are using the Cloud

- Video game makers are using the Cloud

- to deliver _____ to millions of players around the world

- to power real-time fraud _____

- to develop more _____ for patients

Banked Cloze

There is a passage with ten blanks. You are required to select one word for each blank from the list of choices given in a word bank following the passage. Read the passage carefully before making your choices. Each choice in the bank is identified by a letter. Please write the corresponding letter for each item in the blanks. You may not use any of the words in the bank more than once.

What Is the Internet?[3]

NW: 286 GL: 7.8 AWL percentage: 5% Keywords: network; website; online

What is the Internet?

The Internet is the wider network that allows computer networks around the world run by companies, governments, universities and other 1._____ to talk to one another. The result is a mass of cables, computers, data centers, routers, servers, repeaters, satellites, and WiFi towers that allows 2._____ information to travel around the world.

How many people are online?

It depends how you 3._____ it. One metric 4._____ with the International

---

3 From The Guardian website.

Telecommunications Union (ITU)[4], a UN body, counts being online as having used the Internet in the past three months.

It means people are not assumed to use the Internet simply because they live in a town with an Internet cable or near a WiFi tower. By this yardstick, some 3.58 billion people, or 48% of the global 5._____ , were online by the end of 2017. The number should reach 3.8 billion, or 49.2%, by the end of 2018, with half of the world being online by May 2019.

Fixed-line Internet connections are 6._____ in developing countries, so most people connect through their mobile phones. The trend leads to a two-tier experience of the Internet that is hidden by growth figures. What can be done on a mobile phone is a fraction of what can be 7._____ with a desktop, laptop, or tablet, as anyone who has tried to file their tax return on their mobile will know.

"The distinction often gets lost in the discussion around access and 8._____," says Dhanaraj Thakur, research director at the Web Foundation. "We can say that 50% of the world is using the Internet, but the 9._____ are using it on their phones. In terms of productivity, that is 10._____ different from using a desktop or laptop."

A) majority	B) digital	C) organizations
D) population	E) measure	F) strangely
G) slightly	H) popular	I) affordability
J) expensive	K) seldom	L) completely
M) picture	N) achieved	O) minority

4 International Telecommunications Union (ITU): 国际电信联盟，是主管信息通信技术事务的联合国机构，负责分配和管理全球无线电频谱与卫星轨道资源，制定全球电信标准，向发展中国家提供电信援助，促进全球电信发展。

Long Passage

You are going to read a passage with ten statements attached to it. Each statement contains information given in one of the paragraphs. Identify the paragraph from which the information is derived. You may choose a paragraph more than once. Each paragraph is marked with a letter. Please answer the questions by writing the corresponding letter after the statements.

COVID-19 Makes It Clearer than Ever: Access to the Internet Should Be a Universal Right[5]

NW: 1,127   GL: 11.2   **AWL percentage:** 8.02%   Keywords: access; Internet; universal

A   My 100-zip black backpack, previously the logistical and geek centre of my life, now sits neglected in a corner, not needed since COVID-19 abruptly halted my near-constant travel schedule.

B   Life went on—with limited disruption, if not quite as normal. After all, I have enough space, equipment and Internet connectivity to work comfortably from home. In some ways, life has become more efficient. Less jet lag[6]. More sanity.

C   I'm hardly alone in experiencing this. Those of us fortunate to have jobs we can do from home have tidied up our video conference backdrops and changed how we operate.

---

5 From The Guardian website.
6 jet lag: 飞行时差综合征；时差反应

Where they can, many children have adapted, more or less, to virtual classrooms and the need to compete for workspace with their parents.

D   We keep in touch with loved ones via computer screens in ways we couldn't have imagined only three months ago, while the crisis has spawned myriad coping mechanisms—from a boom in online quizzes, art classes and workouts to a golden age for memes.

E   And while many of us are cooped up indoors, we have seen examples of great collective endeavor and support: communities coming together to help each other and the most vulnerable, albeit keeping two meters apart.

F   In all of these things, the web has been the critical unifying force, enabling work, school, social activity and mutual support. Always intended as a platform for creativity and collaboration at a distance, it is great to see it also being used more than ever for compassion at a distance too. This is all very well, of course, if we have the web at our fingertips. But we are the lucky ones. Billions of people don't have the option to turn to the web in times of need or normality. A gross digital divide holds back almost half the planet when it most needs the web.

G   This divide is most acutely experienced in developing countries. The position is particularly dire across Africa, where only one in four people can access the web and the benefits that so many of us take for granted. Women, in particular, in the developing world, are excluded, with men 21% more likely to have online access—rising to 52% in the world's least developed countries.

H   The challenge extends to the wealthiest nations, too: 60,000 children in the UK have no Internet at home and device poverty stops many more from learning online while schools remain closed.

I   In the US, an estimated 12 million children live in homes without broadband connectivity, and people are parking cars outside schools and cafes, desperate for a connection good enough to learn and work "from home". These inequalities fall along the familiar lines of wealth, race and rural urban divides.

J   Working from home isn't an option for many—including some who have jobs that could be done remotely. Businesses in areas without the infrastructure to trade online are denied a lifeline that is keeping others around the world afloat.

K   The Alliance for Affordable Internet[7], an initiative of the World Wide Web

---

7 Alliance for Affordable Internet: 廉价互联网联盟 (A4AI)。A4AI 是由 50 多个成员组成的多元化全球联盟，致力于通过监管与政策改革来降低发展中国家互联网接入的费用。

Foundation[8], which was the foundation that I co-founded with Rosemary Leith, has outlined urgent actions that governments and companies should take to provide this lifeline to more people as quickly as possible.

L　　We're in a world where it is so much harder to get by without the web. And yet the digital divide won't disappear once this crisis is over. The ever-quickening march to digitization has become a sprint. We must make sure those currently in the slow lane have the means to catch up. Otherwise billions will be left behind in the dust. As COVID-19 forces huge change to our lives, we have an opportunity for big, bold action that recognizes that, as with electricity in the last century and postal services before that, the web is an essential utility that governments and business should combine to deliver as a basic right.

M　　History shows us that after all great global upheavals there are major attempts to repair the damage and rebuild, with some more successfully delivered than others. In the midst of this turmoil we must surely strive to ensure some good emerges out of the darkness.

N　　The web can and must be for everyone—now is our moment to make this happen. We have the technical means to connect the entire world in meaningful and affordable ways. We now need the will and the investment.

O　　Governments must lead the way. They must invest in network infrastructure, not only in urban centres, but in rural settings where market forces alone fail to connect residents. And because data affordability remains one of the biggest barriers to access, these networks must be efficient. For example, policies that encourage service providers to share network infrastructure, and regulations designed to shape competitive markets for data, can go a long way towards bringing down costs for users.

P　　And, to connect everyone, governments will need to target typically excluded groups—including people on low incomes, women, and those in rural areas. This means funding public access and digital literacy initiatives to ensure everyone has the skills to use the Internet in meaningful ways.

Q　　Service providers must invest in network performance, reliability and coverage so that everyone is within reach of high-quality connectivity. We have seen experiments with drones, balloons and satellites to connect hard-to-reach areas. While these don't replace good policy and investment in proven technologies, innovation such as this is a welcome in addition to the mix.

8　World Wide Web Foundation: 万维网基金会是由万维网发明者提姆·伯纳斯·李爵士于 2009 年创建的机构，目的是推动开放的万维网作为一种全球公共福利和基本人类权利。

R   There is nothing to stop governments and companies making a choice now, to accelerate progress on connectivity where good changes are happening and to step up where they aren't.

S   Finally, we can all play a role as individuals. If you've relied on the web recently, don't you owe it to the other half of the world to help them get that lifeline, too?

T   Demand action from your government to make universal Internet connectivity a priority. Support a technology NGO[9] such as the World Wide Web Foundation. Back the Contract for the Web—a collaborative project to build a better web, with universal connectivity as a key priority.

U   Just as people campaign for clean water and access to education, we need a global campaign for universal Internet access.

V   We must, of course, be more alert than ever to the web's shortfalls—the privacy violations, the misinformation and the online gender-based violence that has become far too familiar. But these very real problems must not deter us from achieving the foundational challenge of making the web available to all.

W   Just as the world decided that electricity and water were basic needs that should reach everyone, no matter the cost, we should recognize that now is our moment to fight for the web as a basic right. Let's be the generation that delivers universal Internet access.

1. To ensure universal access to high-quality Internet, service providers must invest in network performance, security, and coverage. ☐

2. If one has enough space, facilities, and Internet access to work from home, life could go on as usual. ☐

3. The web is a crucial infrastructure that government policymakers and companies can collaborate to provide as a basic human right. ☐

4. The Alliance for Affordable Internet has outlined immediate steps to ensure that more people have access to the Internet as soon as possible. ☐

5. People on low incomes, women, and those in rural areas are usually excluded groups in disadvantageous position in Internet access. ☐

6. A global campaign for universal Internet access is needed just as campaigns for clean water and access to education. ☐

7. A huge digital divide is stopping nearly half of the population from using the Internet at a time when it is desperately important. ☐

---

9 NGO (Non-Governmental Organizations): 非政府组织

8. Many children have adapted to online education more or less in the COVID-19 period. ☐

9. Even the wealthiest nations like UK have the digital divide challenge, for 60,000 children there have no Internet at home. ☐

10. In the United States, an estimated 12 million children live in households without access to broadband. ☐

Short Passages

There are two passages in this part. Each passage is followed by some questions or unfinished statements. For each passage there are four choices marked A, B, C, and D. You should decide on the best choice and mark the corresponding letter.

Passage one

America's Social Media Addiction Is Getting Worse[10]

NW: 336　GL: 12.0　AWL percentage: 9.91%　Keywords: America; social media; addiction

Facebook users in America spend about 42 minutes a day on the social media platform, according to eMarketer, a research firm. If Josh Hawley has his way, this figure will be capped at 30 minutes. On July 30th the junior senator from Missouri unveiled the "Social Media Addiction Reduction Technology Act", or SMART Act. The bill would limit social media usage to half an hour a day (users would be able to bypass the limit by adjusting their app settings). It would also <u>ban</u> addictive features, such as "infinite scroll" (when a user's entire feed can be seen in one visit) and "autoplay" (when online videos load automatically one after another).

Mr. Hawley's proposal may not go down well with his constituents. A survey in

---

10　From The Economist website.

January and February 2019 from the Pew Research Centre, a think-tank, found that 69% of American adults use Facebook; of these users, more than half visit the site "several times a day". YouTube is even more popular, with 73% of adults saying they watch videos on the platform. For those aged 18 to 24, the figure is 90%. Instagram, a photo-sharing app, is used by 37% of adults. When Pew first conducted the survey in 2012, only a slim majority of Americans used Facebook. Fewer than one in ten had an Instagram account.

Americans are also spending more time than ever on social media sites like Facebook. There is evidence that cutting back on such services might yield health benefits. A paper published last year by Melissa Hunt, Rachel Marx, Courtney Lipson and Jordyn Young, all of the University of Pennsylvania, found that limiting social media usage to 10 minutes a day led to reductions in loneliness, depression, anxiety and fear.

Another paper from 2014 identified a link between heavy social media usage and depression, largely due to a "social comparison" phenomenon, whereby users compare themselves to others and come away with lower evaluations of themselves. Restrictions of the sort proposed by Mr. Hawley might leave addicts better off—at least until the withdrawal sets in.

1. What does the underlined word "ban" (Line 6, Para. 1) mean?

   A. Consent.

   B. Prohibit.

   C. Punish.

   D. Insert.

2. Which statement is NOT true about the SMART Act?

   A. The bill was unveiled by Josh Hawley, a junior senator from Missouri.

   B. The bill would constrain social media usage to 30 minutes per day.

   C. The bill would ban "infinite scroll" when a user's entire feed can be seen in one visit.

   D. Online videos loading automatically one after another is allowed by the bill.

3. Which social media app is not mentioned in the second paragraph?

   A. Facebook.

   B. YouTube.

   C. Twitter.

   D. Instagram.

4. Limiting social media usage to 10 minutes a day led to reductions in the following feelings EXCEPT _____.

   A. anxiety

   B. irritation

   C. depression

   D. loneliness

5. Which statement is true about the paper mentioned in the last paragraph?

   A. It identified a link between moderate social media usage and depression.

   B. Such depression is largely due to a "social comparison" phenomenon.

   C. Users seldom compare themselves to others in social media usage.

   D. By comparing themselves to others, users come away with higher evaluations of themselves.

Passage two

This Is the Online Shopping Mistake You Need to Stop Making Now[11]

NW: 439 GL: 15.2 AWL percentage: 10% Keywords: online; rating; review

Online reviews can be highly entertaining, and theoretically, they should be helping us make good decisions about what to spend our money on. As it turns out, however, they do help us make decisions—just not necessarily the best ones, according to a new study led by Derek Powell, PhD, a Stanford University postdoctoral research fellow. The study was published in Psychological Science, a journal of the Association for Psychological Science.

Specifically, the study reveals that we are more inclined to buy a product that has more reviews than a product that has less, even if the product with more reviews has lower ratings. That inclination is so strong, in fact, that given a choice between two products that have equally bad reviews, we're still inclined to buy the one with more reviews—despite that the higher number of reviews means that the product is even more likely to be bad (because more people agree that it's bad).

Dr. Powell and his colleagues (two from UCLA and one from Indiana University) asked several hundred people to look at a series of cell phone cases, presented in pairs along with the average user rating and number of reviews for each case, and then indicate which case they would be more inclined to purchase. Across the board, for each pair, the participants tended to choose the case that had more reviews, rather than better reviews.

This herd-mentality[12] is a function of social learning, according to Dr. Powell. Social learning is the process by which new behaviors are learned through observing the behavior of others: "The Internet now provides social evidence on an unprecedented scale. However, properly utilizing this evidence requires a capacity for statistical inference[13]."

Pitting "statistical information against social information," the researchers concluded that our brains are so wired to gravitate toward what we see others doing that we find ourselves unable to see beyond that to make meaningful statistical inferences. "We found that people were biased toward choosing to purchase more popular products and that this sometimes led them to make very poor decisions," he explains in a press release by the Association for Psychological Science.

---

11   From Reader's digest website.
12   herd-mentality: 羊群效应；从众心理
13   statistical inference: 统计推理；统计推断

"Consumers try to use information about other people's experiences to make good choices, and retailers have an incentive to steer consumers toward products they will be satisfied with," Dr. Powell added. "Our data suggest that retailers might need to rethink how reviews are presented and consumers might need to do more to educate themselves about how to use reviews to guide their choices." That includes absorbing the notion that a larger number of reviews is not a reliable indicator of a product's quality.

1. According to Paragraph 1, which statement is NOT true about online reviews?

   A. Online reviews do help us make certain decisions.

   B. Online reviews ought to help people make good decisions about what to buy.

   C. Online reviews do help us make best decisions.

   D. Online reviews can be highly entertaining.

2. According to Paragraph 2, which product are we more inclined to buy?

   A. A product that has less reviews than a product that has more reviews.

   B. A product that has more reviews than a product that has less reviews.

   C. A product that has less bad reviews.

   D. A product that has lower ratings.

3. What does the underlined phrase "Across the board" (Line 4, Para.3) mean?

   A. Generally.

   B. Specifically.

   C. Explicitly.

   D. Implicitly.

4. Which is NOT true about the "herd-mentality"?

   A. New behaviors are learned through observing the behavior of others.

   B. The Internet now provides social evidence to follow on an unparalleled scale.

   C. Our minds are hardwired to want to do what we see other people doing.

   D. Properly utilizing social evidence requires a capacity for social inference.

5. **What is Dr. Powell's attitude towards online reviews?**

   A. Positive.

   B. Negative.

   C. Objective.

   D. Indifferent.

Reading Skills

Critical Reading: Evaluating Websites and Text

Here are two more tips that might help you achieve critical reading:

1 Evaluating websites

It is important to remember that ANYONE can create a website or put information on the Web. Therefore, when you are reading articles on the Web, you need to be especially critical. When you are looking for information about a topic on the Web, you may first have to choose among the many sites listed on Google or another search engine.

2 Evaluating text

In addition to evaluating the sources of reading materials, you need to look closely at the text itself to examine the following three aspects.

- Purpose—the reason the writer wrote the text

- Point of view—the writer's position on a particular subject

- Possible bias—how a writer might purposely present ideas or events in ways that favor a particular political or religious belief

Exercises

Please read the above reading skills of critical reading and use the means to finish the following exercises.

1. Use the Internet to find some information about the author of the long passage "COVID-19 Makes It Clearer than Ever: Access to the Internet Should Be a Universal Right". Do you think he or she is qualified to write about this topic and why?

2. What is the author's purpose in writing the article "COVID-19 Makes It Clearer than Ever: Access to the Internet Should Be a Universal Right"?

3. What is the main point of view in the Short Passage Two "This Is the Online Shopping Mistake You Need to Stop Making Now"? Do you agree with it or not?

THINK

Academic Words in Use

Fill in the blanks in the following sentences with the appropriate words provided in the box below. Change the form of the words if necessary.

affordability	addiction	network	review	access
universal	outline	incline	mentality	withdraw

1. I tried to give up smoking several times before I realized I was _____.

2. The President _____ his peace plan for the Middle East.

3. This is a top-quality product at a very _____ price.

4. It is not easy to write a song that has _____ appeal.

5. I can't understand the _____ of people who hurt animals.

6. Following his nervous breakdown, he _____ from public life and refused to give any interviews.

7. Derek writes book _____ for the newspapers.

8. It's important to build up a(n) _____ of professional contacts.

9. You can gain _____ to your records via this website.

10. I am _____ to think that the ancient Greeks understood this better than we do.

Writing

According to a recent study, the more time people use the Internet, the less time they spend with real human beings. Some people say that instead of seeing the Internet as a way of opening new communication possibilities worldwide, we should be concerned about the effect this is having on social interaction.

How far do you agree with this opinion? Write an essay in 30 minutes of 180 words at least and 250 words at most. Please include reasons for your answer and any relevant examples from your own experience or knowledge.

Does the Internet Help or Hurt Social Interaction?

Unit 7 Where Do You Want to Work?

Viewing

More People Considering Moving Out of Expensive Cities if They Can Work Remotely

About the video clip

This video clip discusses why more people are considering moving out of expensive cities if they can work remotely when affected by the spread of COVID-19.

Understanding the video clip

Filling in the blanks

Watch the video clip twice and fill in the blanks.

1. Companies are going to be working _____ long after this pandemic.

2. With so many _____ like Google, Facebook, Dell and Walmart allowing employees to work from home _____, and social distancing the new norm, many city residents are _____ greener pastures.

3. Moves out of New York City to Connecticut, for example, have _____ since April.

4. The median home price in the New York and New Jersey area is _____ dollars, around Nashville _____.

5. When you're living and working in your house, _____ matters even more.

Marking

Now watch the video clip again and mark the box in the second column of the table if they are the reasons mentioned in the video clip why people are considering moving out of expensive cities.

Reasons why people are considering moving out of expensive cities	Mentioned or not
1. Many companies like Google, Facebook, Dell and Walmart allow employees to work from home for some time.	
2. The median home price in small cities is much cheaper than the big cities	
3. Many people necessarily want to escape big cities like New York City.	
4. When you're living and working in your house, extra space matters even more.	
5. It's a good time to move with mortgage rates hitting an all-time low, making buying more affordable.	

Banked Cloze

There is a passage with ten blanks. You are required to select one word for each blank from the list of choices given in a word bank following the passage. Read the passage carefully before making your choices. Each choice in the bank is identified by a letter. Please write the corresponding letter for each item in the blanks. You may not use any of the words in the bank more than once.

The Cities That Supercharge Your Career[1]

NW: 259   GL: 11.0   **AWL percentage:** 7.6%   **Keywords:** cities; talents; high-skill

The International Labour Organization[2] and the Asian Development Bank[3] estimate the 10 countries in the Association of Southeast Asian Nations (ASEAN)[4] will need 14 million more high-skilled workers between 2010 and 2025—a(n) 1._____ of 41%—many of whom will need to be based in the countries' capital cities.

In China, for example, as the economy 2._____ , its major cities are likely to need

---

1 From BBC website.

2 International Labour Organization: 国际劳工组织。该组织是联合国的一个专门机构,简称"劳工组织"。其宗旨是:促进充分就业和提高生活水平;促进劳资双方合作;扩大社会保障措施;保护工人生活与健康。

3 Asian Development Bank(ADB): 亚洲开发银行,简称亚开行或亚行,是一个致力于促进亚洲及太平洋地区发展中成员经济和社会发展的区域性政府间金融开发机构。

4 Association of Southeast Asian Nations(ASEAN): 东南亚国家联盟,简称东盟。1967 年 8 月 8 日成立于泰国曼谷,现有 10 个成员国:印度尼西亚、马来西亚、菲律宾、泰国、新加坡、文莱、柬埔寨、老挝、缅甸、越南。

people with skills in services and technology, rather than the 3. _____ manufacturing of the past. Global recruiters expect cyber security, big data, digital analytics and finance technology to be among the most in-demand 4._____ , as the government moves ahead with plans to make Shanghai a(n) 5. _____ for tech innovation.

"The best locations to develop a career will be those where there is the greatest demand for 6. _____ ," says Mario Ferraro, who heads the global mobility practice for Asia, Middle East, Africa and Turkey at Mercer, an international consultancy. "It all comes down to the basic laws of economic 7. _____ and demand."

The scramble for skills has prompted some countries, and even cities, to develop special programme for expats and entrepreneurs, hoping to 8. _____ the most talented people to their shores.

In 2010, China started streamlining red tape with its Thousand Talents Plan to encourage skilled foreigners to work at leading universities and institutes. Malaysia offers 9. _____ residence visas to "foreign talent", allowing certain professionals to stay and work in the country for as long as 10 years, while the Netherlands started its Epicenter in 2008 to help 10. _____ working in Amsterdam and its surrounding areas.

A) talent	B) expands	C) center
D) increase	E) admits	F) lure
G) career	H) areas	I) alternative
J) supply	K) long-term	L) technology
M) foreigners	N) healthcare	O) low-skilled

Long Passage

You are going to read a passage with ten statements attached to it. Each statement contains information given in one of the paragraphs. Identify the paragraph from which the information is derived. You may choose a paragraph more than once. Each paragraph is marked with a letter. Please answer the questions by writing the corresponding letter after the statements.

What Location Is Better for Your Career? How to Choose Between a Growth Market and an Affordable City[5]

NW: 1,097 GL: 10.4 **AWL percentage:** 7.83% **Keywords:** career; location; move

A   A recent graduate who wants to land at a tech company is considering a move from a suburb to San Francisco[6]. A mid-career professional who wants to trade his big corporate role for something more entrepreneurial is considering a move from pricey New York City[7] to Seattle[8] or Denver[9]. There are pros and cons when you are choosing

---

5 From Forbes website.
6 San Francisco: 旧金山，又译"三藩市""圣弗朗西斯科"，美国加利福尼亚州太平洋沿岸港口城市，世界著名旅游胜地、加州（人口）第四大城市。
7 New York City: 纽约，是纽约都会区的核心，也是美国最大城市，同时也是世界最大的城市之一。
8 Seattle: 西雅图，位于美国华盛顿州西北部的太平洋沿岸。
9 Denver: 丹佛市县（City and County of Denver），美国科罗拉多州的一个合并市县，也是科罗拉多州的首府和最大城市。

between an expensive growth market, like NYC, San Francisco or D.C., or a more affordable, smaller city like Seattle, Denver or Philadelphia[10].

B   Which location is better for your career? The answer depends on several factors, both personal and professional. Here are six questions to consider when choosing the best location for your next career move:

1 - How much flexibility do you have to choose?

C   The recent graduate I mentioned in the opening ultimately stayed where he was (and still landed in tech) because his spouse had just started a three-year commitment to a job in the area. Sure, they could have decided to have a commuter marriage for several years, but they both didn't want that. At the start of his job search, this very ambitious MBA burned a lot of emotional energy lamenting his lack of proximity to the biggest tech markets. However, once he empowered himself with the knowledge that staying in a smaller market was something he chose, he was able to refocus his energy and land at a fast-growth start-up right where he was.

D   Before you drive yourself crazy wishing you were somewhere else, confirm that location is actually an option. You may be worrying about a hypothetical decision that will never have to be made.

2 - How important is where you live versus other factors?

E   An HR colleague of mine actually did have the flexibility to move and ultimately did move. She was in the finance industry in NYC, so arguably the global capital for her career path, but with two young children and a spouse who could work from anywhere, she opted for a smaller city in-between both sets of grandparents. This was as much a professional move as a personal one. With the additional nearby resources, she could travel more and work more unpredictable hours, which enabled her to take a bigger role than what she initially had.

F   Though some locations seem more supportive to certain careers (NYC is almost synonymous with finance), depending on your own circumstances, you might need a different kind of support and therefore prioritize other factors, like my colleague above or this young professional who left a six-figure job to move closer to family.

3 - Can you afford to move?

G   You may not be in a financial position to move. I once hired a recent graduate

---

10   Philadelphia: 费城，位于美国宾夕法尼亚州东南部，是特拉华河谷都会区的中心城市。费城是美国最老、最
     具历史意义的城市之一，1790—1800 年，在华盛顿建市前曾是美国的首都，因此在美国史上有非常重要的地位。

for a low-paying, entry-level position. She had an excellent business background and could have found a spot anywhere, but here she was in NYC, one of the most expensive locations to start a career. However, she lived at home and had a large extended family[11], so she didn't have to cook her own meals for years. She saved up enough money to buy her own place within a few years. The personal support also enabled her to really focus on her career, where she leapfrogged into management with several quick promotions.

H   Don't dismiss an expensive market just because you are starting out. It may be within reach if you tap personal connections, and the growth opportunities can help you make back your investment more quickly.

4 - Is now the best time to change locations?

I   I once coached a finance executive, who at the peak of his career, left a great job in a growth market to relocate to a small town and help out his elderly parents. Because his hometown is rural (it wasn't even a suburb) there is no way he would be able to replicate his role in his new location. However, he was able to time his move around the completion of a key initiative for his group and the hiring of his successor. In return, he negotiated a large severance and some consulting work while he is gone.

J   The right timing can make a difficult move more palatable. This finance executive figured out how to move from big to small without taking a big hit. On the flip side, if you want to move from low-cost to expensive, you can look for a role that takes the bigger expenses into account.

5 - Is your career path the only one to consider?

K   If you are in a dual-career household[12], how will you decide if a relocation opportunity arises for one of you? I once worked at a recruiting firm where a job search almost fell apart because the position required relocation, and the new hire assumed her spouse was on board with a move, but at the eleventh hour, he decided not to come. (It wasn't my project, but last I heard of it, they were in marriage counseling!)

L   Don't spend too much time imagining the ideal location for your career before you clear it with any other decision-makers who will influence a go/no decision. In addition to a spouse, children or extended family may weigh more heavily than you expect.

6 - Does your ideal career require a move?

M   If you want to work in the headquarters of a Fortune 50 company, you have to be in

---

11   extended family: 大家庭（几代同堂的家庭）
12   dual-career household: 双职工家庭

a city that hosts one of these companies. Some industries are tied very closely to specific areas (e.g., energy and Houston, film and Los Angeles). Or, you might be at a global company that asks you to relocate. This was the case with an operations professional I coached who was happily and successfully working at a major metro in the Middle East but was being asked to transfer to a small city in Italy. It was a key initiative for the company and a significant step-up in responsibility.

N   Depending on how your career unfolds and what your priorities are, sometimes your career path leads you somewhere different from where you are. Your personal location preference may need to take a back seat to professional requirements, depending on the career you choose. Sometimes global careers require moves from big to small locations depending on what works for the company.

O   You can build, grow, maintain and even pivot your career in either a growth market or an affordable city.

P   Location is never the only consideration in a career decision, and depending on personal and professional factors, you can probably nurture your career wherever you prefer to live.

1. Make sure the location you want to work in is a practical option. ☐

2. Location is in no way the only thing to weigh in a profession decision. ☐

3. Your personal preferences for location may give way to professional demands. ☐

4. Both a boom market and a low-cost city can be the place in which you can build and further your career. ☐

5. A right timing can make a tough move more bearable. ☐

6. The choice of the best job location is closely related with a number of personal and professional considerations. ☐

7. Checking with other decision-makers is also important. ☐

8. You should weigh pros and cons when choosing to move between an expensive large market and an low-cost but smaller city. ☐

9. Financial situation can be a factor influencing your decision to relocate your job. ☐

10. If you are able to tap your personal connections, working in an expensive market might be feasible. ☐

Short Passages

There are two passages in this part. Each passage is followed by some questions or unfinished statements. For each passage there are four choices marked A, B, C, and D. You should decide on the best choice and mark the corresponding letter.

Passage one

Working in the Greater Bay Area Helps with Your Career Planning[13]

NW: 406 GL: 12.8 AWL percentage: 6.08%
Keywords: Greater Bay Area; career; development

Looking for a job is like drawing on a blank piece of paper. You might be <u>at a loss</u> about how to draw the picture. Nonetheless, there are plenty of possibilities. When Hong Kong people explore the abundant job opportunities in the Mainland cities of the Greater Bay Area[14] (GBA), it is like drawing a picture on a much larger piece of paper with a lot more colors to choose from.

---

13 From talent.gov.hk website.

14 Greater Bay Area: 粤港澳大湾区（英文名 Guangdong-Hong Kong-Macao Greater Bay Area，缩写 GBA）由香港、澳门两个特别行政区和广东省广州、深圳、珠海、佛山、惠州、东莞、中山、江门、肇庆九个珠三角城市组成，是中国开放程度最高、经济活力最强的区域之一。

KPMG[15] China, HSBC[16] and Hong Kong General Chamber of Commerce[17] jointly published a survey report called "Exploring the GBA" in early 2020. The survey polled 747 senior executives of large and medium-sized enterprises from various sectors from the Mainland, Hong Kong and Macau to understand their views on the outlook for the GBA. The results showed that these companies were generally optimistic about the future development of the GBA.

GBA will grow faster than other Mainland cities

About 80% of the respondents expected that the GBA's economy would grow faster than other Mainland cities in the next three years. They generally believed that the development of the GBA would drive robust revenue growth for their companies. Around 56% of the respondents expected a revenue growth of at least 20% in the next three years, and 23% of them expected a revenue growth of more than 30%. Considering the enormous growth potential of the GBA in the next few years, over half (52%) of the respondents said that they planned to expand their businesses in the GBA before 2022.

Working in the GBA is beneficial to your career development

Besides, over 13% of the respondents believed that at least half of their senior officers would station in more than one GBA city in the next three years. Over 30% (34%) of the companies located in the Mainland cities of the GBA believed that more than half of their senior officers would station in more than one GBA city, suggesting that talent investments in the GBA would keep increasing in the next few years. More and more senior managers would station in the GBA, implying that life or work experience in the GBA would become a basic condition for senior officers. If young people want to advance their careers, they should step out of their comfort zone[18] as early as possible, and try to live and work in different cities of the GBA with a view to building connections and solid foundation for their future career development.

15　KPMG: 毕马威成立于 1897 年，总部位于荷兰阿姆斯特丹，是一家网络遍布全球的专业服务机构，专门提供审计、税务和咨询等服务。

16　HSBC: 汇丰银行，全称香港上海汇丰银行有限公司（The Hongkong and Shanghai Banking Corporation Limited）。

17　Hong Kong General Chamber of Commerce: 香港总商会

18　comfort zone: 舒适区，放松区（指人自我放松、不追求高效益的状态）

1. What does the underlined phrase "at a loss" (Line 1, Para. 1) mean?

   A. Hopeless.　　B. Clueless.　　C. Worthless.　　D. Priceless.

2. "It is like drawing a picture on a much larger piece of paper with a lot more colors to choose from" (Para. 1) means_____

   A. It is easier to draw a picture with larger piece of paper and more colours to choose from.

   B. Greater Bay Area covers larger lands and thus has more job opportunities.

   C. Job opportunities in the Greater Bay Area are abundant and various to explore.

   D. Hong Kong people prefer to hunt jobs in Mainland cities of the Greater Bay Area.

3. Which one does NOT support the idea that GBA will grow faster than other Mainland cities?

   A. About 80% of the respondents expected that the GBA's economy would grow faster than other Mainland cities in the next three years.

   B. More than half of the respondents expected a revenue growth of at least 20% in the next three years.

   C. 23% of the respondents expected a revenue growth of more than 50%.

   D. Over half of the respondents planned to expand their businesses in the GBA before 2022.

4. Which one is true according to the last paragraph?

   A. Over 30% of the respondents believed that at least half of their senior officers would station in more than one GBA city in the next three years.

   B. Talent investments in the GBA would keep the same level in the next few years.

   C. Life or work experience in the GBA would become a basic condition for junior officers.

   D. Live and work in different cities of the GBA may help build connections and foundation for future career development.

5. What do most respondents think of the prospect of working in Greater Bay Area?

   A. Indifferent.

   B. Optimistic.

C. Uncertain.

D. Gloomy.

Passage two

Working from Home:
Why the Office Will Never Be the Same[19]

NW: 416 GL: 10.5 **AWL percentage:** 5.21% **Keywords:** remote work; home; revolution

In the *Before Time*, Dan O'Leary, a director of business partnerships at a tech company, commuted two to three hours a day and flew on weekly business trips. He adhered to a strict schedule: his alarm was set for 5:30 a.m. to fit in a Peloton[20] ride and shower before catching the train, and his workdays were <u>jammed</u> with meetings.

Since the coronavirus upended office life in March, his workdays have been very different, even idyllic. Sometimes he works from a picnic blanket in a park near his home in San Jose, Calif., or calls into meetings while on a walk. He is working about the same number of hours, usually 50 a week, but said he is more creative and productive because he gets to choose his schedule. As a manager, he is letting his team do the same. "I don't need to see them at their desk at 6 p.m.," he said. "I can review their work at 10 o'clock at night, sitting in bed after my Netflix[21] binge."

His Peloton miles have doubled to 700 a month because he cycles midday or during meetings (though he no longer keeps his video on during rides; his co-workers banned it). His marriage has benefited from being able to eat lunch with his wife. He stopped having nightmares about missing business flights, and he sleeps 40 more minutes a night.

Mr. O'Leary is among the most privileged workers. His job is secure, it's easily done from home, he can afford the space and technology to do it remotely, and his company is supportive. He's not alone: many white-collar workers say their lives are now like Mr. O'Leary's. They have adjusted their schedules to better fit their lives, and they're enjoying it, according to a new, nationally representative survey by Morning Consult for *The New York Times*.

This is exactly the revolution that many workers—and those who study them—have

---

19 From The New York Times website.

20 Peloton: 一个美国互动健身平台。

21 Netflix: 美国奈飞公司，简称网飞。是一家会员订阅制的流媒体播放平台，总部位于美国加利福尼亚州洛斯盖图。

been envisioning for years: giving people control over where and when work gets done, instead of demanding face time at the office and rewarding those who spend the longest hours there.

It's clear that America's workers actually like the new way of doing things, even amid the challenges of the pandemic. In the survey by *The Times* and Morning Consult, which polled 1,123 people who have worked at home these past few months—representing the range of jobs, demographics and income levels of America's remote workers—86 percent said they were satisfied with remote work.

1. **What does the underlined word "jammed" (Line 4, Para. 1) mean?**

   A. Blocked.

   B. Full.

   C. Absent.

   D. Arranged.

2. **What can we infer from the second paragraph?**

   A. Dan O'Leary's working style is similar to that of days before COVID-19 hit.

   B. Dan O'Leary is working much less number of hours nowadays.

   C. Dan O'Leary enjoys more flexibility in working arrangement than before.

   D. Dan O'Leary has the privilege to choose his schedule as a manager while his team members cannot do so.

3. **Remote working has brought many changes to Dan O'Leary's lifestyle EXCEPT _____ .**

   A. he can spare more time to do physical exercises

   B. his marriage has benefited from being able to eat lunch with his wife

   C. he no longer has nightmares about missing business meeting

   D. he sleeps longer than before

4. **Which is the revolution that many workers have been imagining for years?**

   A. The managers decide the working style.

   B. Face-to face time is strictly required at the office.

   C. Those who spend the longest hours in office are rewarded.

   D. The workers are able to decide where and when work gets done.

5. The survey by *The Times* and Morning Consult shows that the attitude of many America's workers towards remote work is _____.

   A. supportive

   B. objective

   C. indifferent

   D. sympathetic

Reading Skills

Annotating

Annotating a text is when the reader "marks up" a text to indicate places of importance or something they don't understand. Careful annotating allows you both to read actively and to pull out the essential ideas at the same time. The annotations reflect a range of ways of responding to and engaging with a text: noting questions, arguing, agreeing, reflecting, speculating, and making connections. Because annotating is a deeply personal experience, your own annotations to any text will likely differ.

Annotating is sometimes called "reading with a pencil in your hand", so the first step in reflecting upon a text is to read it with a pencil or a pen in hand (or a computer at the ready).

As you annotate, focus on some or all of the following:

Definitions: Look up and write down definitions of unfamiliar words.

Concepts: Underline what you think are the most important, interesting, or difficult concepts.

Tone: Note the writer's tone—sarcastic, sincere, witty, shrill, etc.

Biases: Look out for the writer's biases and unstated assumptions (and your own).

Responses: Ask questions and note your own reactions and insights.

Connections: Make connections with other texts you have read or your own experiences.

Exercises

Please fill in the blanks with words or sentences according to the given paragraph in the annotations column.

Annotations	Paragraph
1. _____ *n.* the ability to change or be changed easily to suit a different situation 2. _____ *v.* to choose one thing or do one thing instead of another 3. The factor influencing her choice for a smaller city in-between both sets of grandparents: _____ _____ _____ 4. This was as much a _____ move as a _____ one. 5. The outcome of her choice of working location: _____ _____ _____	**2 - How important is where you live versus other factors?** An HR colleague of mine actually did have the flexibility to move and ultimately did move. She was in the finance industry in NYC, so arguably the global capital for her career path, but with two young children and a spouse who could work from anywhere, she opted for a smaller city in-between both sets of grandparents. This was as much a professional move as a personal one. With the additional nearby resources, she could travel more and work more unpredictable hours, which enabled her to take a bigger role than what she initially had. (Extracted from Long Passage in this unit)

THINK

Academic Words in Use

Fill in the blanks in the following sentences with the appropriate words provided in the box below. Change the form of the words if necessary.

talent	innovation	high-skilled	flexibility	commitment
career	executive	adjust	envision	revolution

1. There is a relative shortage of _____ laborer and surplus of low-skilled laborer.

2. The company has shown that it can attract and retain top _____.

3. She gave up a promising _____ in advertising in order to look after her children.

4. All the latest technological _____ of cinema were used to create the special effects.

5. She is now a senior _____, having worked her way up through the company.

6. The new law gives auto makers more _____ in meeting lower pollution targets.

7. As a teacher you have to _____ your methods to suit the needs of slower children.

8. The government reaffirmed its _____ to the peace process.

9. Computers have _____ the way we work.

10. He _____ a day when every household will have access to the Internet.

Writing

For this part, you are allowed 30 minutes to read the following paragraphs and continue writing to make it a well-structured article. You should write at least 180 words but no more than 250 words.

Should a Career Be Started in a Big City or a Small City?

It's easy to be attracted to the idea of a big city—fast-paced, brightly-lit—the perfect setting for one's burning ambitions. But what if moving to the big city isn't the only way to find success? In fact, small cities and regional areas can also have advantages for one's career.

First of all, smaller areas are more likely to have a shortage of qualified professionals, which can help a specialist shine.

Unit **8** Online Education

Viewing

Common Misconceptions about Distance Learning

About the video clip

This video clip discusses 7 common misconceptions students have about distance learning.

Understanding the video clip

Fill in the blanks in the table below.

Misconceptions	Realities
1. Online classes are easier than traditional classes.	Online courses are as hard or even more challenging than traditional courses. For example, in addition to typical classroom activities like readings, test, and papers, online courses also have _____, such as discussion board postings, collaborative projects, and game-based activities. Whereas face-to-face courses might meet just two times a week and require _____, online courses often require students to complete activities _____, and all students will be required to contribute.

2. Online courses take less time than traditional courses.	The reality is that an online course can take _____ time as a traditional course. You need to log in frequently and stay engaged to keep yourself _____.
3. I can work entirely at my own pace.	Online classes still _____. You'll have to show up at specific times or places to participate, thus you'll need to be _____ and you'll need to manage your time well.
4. I won't get to know the other students very well in an online course.	Good online courses help you develop similar relationships to those you have in face-to-face courses. Through icebreakers, self-introductions, _____ and collaborative assignments you will get to know your classmates well. If you feel shy in a face-to-face classroom, you may even have an easier time _____ other students in an online class.
5. I won't get individual attention from my professor.	You will have access to help when you need it. Initiate a conversation with you professor and let them know when you're _____.
6. I won't learn as much in an online course.	Good online courses can accomplish the same _____ as traditional face-to-face courses with high levels of engagement.
7. Online degrees don't carry the respect of traditional college degrees.	Online curriculum is the same that you would learn in campus-based courses and shares the same prestigious accreditation, the only difference is _____.

Further thoughts

The prevalence of distance learning has triggered a continuous wave of animated discussion over its benefits and drawbacks. List some of them in the table below.

Benefits of distance learning	Drawbacks of distance learning
1. It's flexible.	1. It is difficult to stay motivated.
2. It improves computer skills.	2. It has no physical interaction.
…	…

Banked Cloze

There is a passage with ten blanks. You are required to select one word for each blank from the list of choices given in a word bank following the passage. Read the passage carefully before making your choices. Each choice in the blank is identified by a letter. Please write the corresponding letter for each item in the blanks. You may not use any of the words in the bank more than once.

Online Tutoring Works Better than Some Might Expect[1]

NW: 297   GL: 7.6   AWL percentage: 1.98%   Keywords: VIPKid; online tutoring; lesson

Amanda Spikes, aged 27, sits in her tiny bedroom in Brooklyn, New York, talking through her headset to eight-year-old Joey in Hebei Province, northern China. On the wall behind her are 1._____ that read "Team Amanda" and "VIPKid[2]", the company for which she works. On the screen are images of her, Joey and some 2._____ materials.

"Happy New Year, Joey!" says Ms. Spikes, enunciating very clearly. Then she sings him a little song: "I like food, I like fruit, fruit tastes good in the morning," and claps when Joey 3._____ it. This lesson is going better than the last one, when Joey messed up the 4._____ by licking the iPad screen.

---

1 From The Economist website.
2 VIPKid: 一家网络在线教育公司。学生和老师通过其视频聊天平台进行学习交流。

VIPKid is the biggest of a number of companies using technology to provide teachers in the West for Asian children who want to learn English. Its 60,000 teachers are 5._____ people with classroom experience who prefer the freelance life.

Online tutoring works better than older people might expect. Nine-year-old Zhang Yutong in Tianjin wasn't making much 6._____ in her 30-strong class at school; now, says her mother, "I feel she is 7._____ happy when she talks to VIPKid's tutors. She is quite willing to express herself." Yutong's teacher, Jessica, asks her to propose a(n) 8._____ ending to the gentle tale of Miss Snowball's cat. "The cat could die," says Yutong cheerfully, making them both laugh.

Ms. Spikes says she has a better connection with her online pupils than she did when teaching an actual classroom-full of them in South Korea: "I feel really 9._____ in these little kids." Her youngest pupil, astonishingly, is three. "Getting her to make the right sounds is a really big thing," she says. But she 10._____ that the parents face a bigger challenge, just getting the child to sit still.

A) mostly	B) invested	C) progress
D) truly	E) admits	F) resources
G) lost	H) active	I) alternative
J) teaching	K) strangely	L) technology
M) repeats	N) hangings	O) hopes

Long Passage

You are going to read a passage with ten statements attached to it. Each statement contains information given in one of the paragraphs. Identify the paragraph from which the information is derived. You may choose a paragraph more than once. Each paragraph is marked with a letter. Please answer the questions by writing the corresponding letter after the statements.

This Company May Hold the Secret to the Future of Education[3]

NW: 987   GL: 10.6   AWL percentage: 5.21%

Keywords: Luis von Ahn; Duolingo; online learning

A   Luis von Ahn, the co-founder and CEO of language learning service Duolingo, says MOOCs[4] make little sense for the digital world. Luis von Ahn runs what is arguably the hottest educational tool online at the moment, but he's also a computer science professor at Carnegie Mellon University.

B   Even he admits that lectures, especially delivered via webcast, can be pretty boring. "You take a lecture that's not all that great and put it on video, it's actually going to be

---

3 From TIME website.

4 MOOC (massive open online course): 慕课是一种旨在通过网络实现无限制参与和开放访问的在线课程。

worse," he says. "Typically, the things that succeed the most online are the things that are better online than offline. Think about email versus mail."

C   Luis von Ahn believes he has developed a platform that can indeed be better online—and on smartphones. Duolingo, which turns two years old this week, offers bite-sized lessons in French, Spanish, English and several other languages for beginners and intermediate-level speakers.

D   Users learn vocabulary words, grammatical structures and even proper pronunciation by speaking into their device's microphone. The service guides students through a battery of challenges, awarding points and badges for correct answers. Users can compete with friends who are learning the same languages.

E   The concept of learning a new language through software is hardly revolutionary, but it's Duolingo's mobile app that sets it apart. Six months into the company's existence, Duolingo had 300,000 active users, all on its website. In the year and a half since it launched a mobile app for iOS, that number has leapt to 13 million, more than MOOC platforms Udacity, edX and Coursera combined, according to usage figures released by those firms. 85% of these users are learning with the mobile app, which Apple named the App of the Year in 2013.

F   "One of the main ways to deliver education over the next 10 to 20 years is going to be through smartphones," Luis von Ahn says. "It's the only way that this actually can scale. This is why we put so much effort into our apps as opposed to our website."

G   The mobile approach has advantages both in the developed world—it's easier to commit to a quick language lesson during lunch than block off an hour after work to sit at a desktop computer—and in emerging markets, where many people use smartphones as their primary computing device. "About 1 to 2 billion people do not have access to very good education," Luis von Ahn says, "but hundreds of millions of these people are very soon or already have access to smartphones."

H   The son of two medical doctors, Luis von Ahn grew up in Guatemala, a country with one of the lowest literacy rates in the world. He says Duolingo, which is free and doesn't have advertising, is primarily aimed at those people who can't afford to take a college course or buy expensive software like Rosetta Stone[5]. "We've become zealots about providing free education," he says. "We develop for the poor people."

I   And yet, Duolingo is a for-profit business. To make money, the company gets its

---

5 Rosetta Stone: 罗塞达石碑，于 1799 年发现于罗塞达，上刻埃及象形文字、通俗字和希腊文，从而成为解读埃及文字的钥匙。本文中意为如师通语言学习软件。

users to translate real news articles from sites like CNN[6] and Buzzfeed[7] into their native languages as a way to practice their English. Duolingo then charges these sites between two and three cents per word for the translations. von Ahn says the venture generates hundreds of thousands of dollars in revenue per year, but Duolingo is not profitable. The company just began offering an English language proficiency test for $20 aimed at job seekers, but it's not yet clear how many employers will accept a Duolingo certification as an alternative to more established (and expensive) programs. The company has raised $38 million in venture funding.

J Whether people are actually learning new languages effectively with Duolingo is still an open question. Luis von Ahn is careful not to oversell the capabilities of the service. The idea that a piece of software could make a person fluent in a foreign language in mere hours is, in his words, "bull—t." "If you really want to become perfectly fluent, probably what you need to do is move to that country," he says. "Learning a language is something that takes years." Still, he says completing all the lessons in a language course in Duolingo is about the equivalent of taking an intermediate-level language course in college. A study commissioned by the company found that people learned as much taking Duolingo lessons in Spanish for 34 hours as they would in a semester of an introductory college class.

K That doesn't mean that apps are going to replace classrooms anytime soon. Though there's great potential in educational tools built for the Web and for mobile, their usefulness varies greatly by subject, says Matthew Chingos, a fellow at the Brown Center on Education Policy at the Brookings Institution. "If I want to learn about the history of the Ottoman Empire[8], it's harder to imagine the really engaging version of that where you're doing one-sentence interactions around a topic like that," he says. "Is this going to replace the way things are done now? I don't think it is. But can these tools be important supplements? I think they can."

L Duolingo, along with other web-native learning tools like the computer programming site Codecademy[9], have carved out an online learning experience that feels both simpler and more engaging than the typical MOOC, which essentially replicates the college lecture hall.

M Luis von Ahn plans to focus on improving Duolingo's adaptive learning capabilities, so that no two users will have the exact same lesson plan. The goal, he says, is for the app to perform more like a well-trained personal tutor than a pedantic professor.

---

6 CNN (Cable News Network): 有线电视新闻网是一个总部设在美国亚特兰大的跨国新闻付费电视频道。
7 BuzzFeed: 一家美国网络媒体、新闻和娱乐公司，专注于数字媒体。
8 the Ottoman Empire: 奥斯曼帝国
9 Codecademy: 一家在线学习编程的网站。

Eventually, he sees Duolingo's interactive learning experiences spreading to many other subjects. "A really good one-on-one tutor can teach a 10-year-old kid algebra in six months," he says. "I think an app should be able to do that."

1. Duolingo is a platform that offers lessons of various languages to its users. ☐

2. Duolingo has undergone a phenomenal growth in the number of its users. ☐

3. Duolingo gains revenue by its translation business with news websites. ☐

4. Duolingo is intent on bringing free education to people with limited means. ☐

5. Duolingo helps learners to improve their language learning through challenges and competitions. ☐

6. Although Duolingo cannot make fluent speakers, it can be a good help. ☐

7. Duolingo is attractive both in the developed countries and in the developing countries. ☐

8. Duolingo is better than MOOC in seizing the attention of its users. ☐

9. Duolingo will provide language learners with customized courses. ☐

10. Duolingo can be an important support tool for classroom learning. ☐

Short Passages

There are two passages in this part. Each passage is followed by some questions or unfinished statements. For each passage there are four choices marked A, B, C, and D. You should decide on the best choice and mark the corresponding letter.

Passage one

Can Online Courses Keep Students from Cheating?[10]

NW: 389   GL: 13.2   AWL percentage: 8.21%
Keywords: Coursera; cheating; remote proctoring

From the beginning, MOOC providers have struggled with the issue of cheating. In August, several professors teaching Coursera courses complained of various forms of cheating in their classes. Some students had <u>plagiarized</u> essays, some had illicitly collaborated on exams, some had posted solutions to test questions online or e-mailed answers to classmates.

In response, Coursera, which has nearly three dozen major university partners, instituted an honor code; every time students submit coursework, they have to check a box that says, "In accordance with the Honor Code, I certify that my answers here are

---

10   From TIME website.

my own work, and that I have appropriately acknowledged all external sources (if any) that were used in this work." The company is also working on integrating antiplagiarism software. "We saw that we needed to do a better job of communicating to students what we consider acceptable academic standards," said Andrew Ng, a Stanford professor and one of Coursera's co-founders.

Some higher-tech options on the table include a system of remote proctoring, currently under development at Coursera, in which students place their passport or other identification card in front of their webcam and then begin taking the test while a human proctor somewhere in the world observes them. This wouldn't stop all cheating— what's to stop a friend from sitting outside the camera's field of vision and mouthing answers to the test taker? —But remote proctoring could act as a restraint. The Georgia Institute of Technology[11], which received a Gates Foundation[12] grant to develop three introductory-level MOOCs in English composition, psychology and physics, is considering incorporating high-tech authentication processes for these courses, including retina scans and facial-recognition software.

But cracking down on would-be cheaters will not only cost money, it could also restrict the original intent of MOOCs, which was to provide educational opportunities to all, just for the sake of learning. "It's not necessarily ideal," said Coursera's Ng. "But the world seems to be moving toward test-based granting of credit."

He's worried that designing courses with cheating in mind will cause MOOCs to lose too much of their openness. "We can't get too crazy about cheating," he said. "We have to accept the fact that we can't keep this thing airtight, and the more we try to make it airtight, the worse it becomes as an educational experience. Cheating is not something you can eliminate."

1. **What does the underlined word "plagiarized" (Line 3, Para. 1) mean?**

    A. Copied.

    B. Coauthored.

    C. Sold.

    D. Published.

11　The Georgia Institute of Technology: 佐治亚理工学院也被简称为 Georgia Tech，是位于美国亚特兰大市的一所综合性公立大学。

12　Gates Foundation: 盖茨基金会创建于 2000 年，是由比尔·盖茨与美琳达·盖茨夫妇资助的全球最大的慈善基金会。

2. **What can we infer from the second paragraph?**

   A. The use of an honor code will hardly improve academic honesty.

   B. Coursera has underestimated the effectiveness of antiplagiarism software.

   C. Coursera is seeking help from more than 30 universities to handle online cheating.

   D. Coursera had failed to demonstrate to students academic standards acceptable to it.

3. **What could be the impact of remote proctoring?**

   A. Holding students back from cheating in exams.

   B. Changing the way exams are to be taken in the future.

   C. Making online exams as formal and airtight as offline ones.

   D. Driving test takers to invite a friend to mouth answers to them.

4. **What is the author's attitude towards the efforts to stops cheating?**

   A. Supportive.

   B. Objective.

   C. Indifferent.

   D. Sympathetic.

5. **What is worrying Andrew Ng?**

   A. Cheating has turned out to be a necessary evil.

   B. MOOC providers cannot eliminate cheating once and for all.

   C. Focusing too much on cheating may lead MOOCs away from their openness.

   D. The world is attaching too much importance to a test-based evaluation system.

Massive Open Online Forces[13]

NW: 419   GL: 11.5   AWL percentage: 7.94%
Keywords: MOOCs; universities; marginal cost

In America, bowing to the inevitable, universities have joined various startups in the rush to provide stand-alone instruction online, through Massive Open Online Courses, or MOOCs. Though much experimentation lies ahead, economics can <u>shed light on</u> how the market for higher education may change.

Two big forces underpin a university's costs. The first is the need for physical proximity. Adding students is expensive—they require more buildings and instructors—and so a university's marginal cost[14] of production is high. It is also hard to raise productivity. University lecturers can teach at most a few hundred students each semester.

MOOCs work completely differently. The most notable feature of the online course is its rock-bottom marginal cost: teaching additional students is virtually free. Having invested in the production of a course, a provider's incentive is to sell it to as many students as possible. After the initial cost is covered, each additional unit sold is pure profit. A low price maximizes registrations and profit. But as prices converge towards marginal cost, there will be little scope for undercutting winner-take-all, "superstar" competitions. The best courses attract the most customers and profit handsomely as a result. In this respect, online education may more closely resemble information industries such as film-making than service industries such as hair-cutting.

Caroline Hoxby, an economist at Stanford University, argues that MOOCs threaten different universities in different ways. Less selective institutions are close substitutes for MOOCs. Course content is often standardized and interaction with professors is limited in order to keep costs down. Students generally pay the cost of their education themselves and upfront, but drop-out rates are nonetheless high. MOOCs can provide a similar experience with more flexibility and at much less cost.

Elite institutions face very different circumstances, Ms. Hoxby reckons. They operate like venture-capital firms, offering subsidized, labor-intensive education to

---

13   From The Economist website.

14   marginal cost: 在经济学里，边际成本指的是每增产一单位的产品，总成本所产生的变化；即，增产一单位商品的成本。

highly qualified students. They aim to cultivate a sense of belonging and gratitude in students in order to recoup their investment decades later in the form of donations from successful alumni.

Ironically, these universities may have threatened their own business model by embracing MOOCs. Online courses break the personal link between students and university and, if offered cheaply to outsiders, may make regular graduates feel more like chumps than the chosen few. For top schools, the best bet may simply be to preserve their exclusivity.

1. **What does the underlined phrase "shed light on" (Line 3, Para. 1) mean?**

   A. Conclude.　　B. Explain.　　C. Prove.　　D. Record.

2. **What can we learn from Paragraph 3?**

   A. Online education differs from hair-cutting in its production cost.

   B. Neither MOOCs nor film-making industry cares about high marginal costs.

   C. Online education should not be considered as an information industry.

   D. Competition in online education may shift its focus from price to quality.

3. **How do MOOCs threaten less selective institutions according to Caroline Hoxby?**

   A. By allowing students to learn first and pay later.

   B. By decreasing the flexibility of their course content.

   C. By setting a highly competitive price for their courses.

   D. By offering more online interaction with their professors.

4. **What do elite institutions aim to do according to Caroline Hoxby?**

   A. They aim to transform their current business model.

   B. They aim to create joint ventures with their alumni.

   C. They aim to profit from their successful students.

   D. They aim to subsidize less qualified students.

5. **What does the author think of the future of top schools?**

   A. Gloomy but still hopeful.

   B. Promising and prosperous.

   C. Uncertain and unforeseeable.

   D. Fine but eventful.

Reading Skills

Summarizing a Whole Passage

Summarizing a whole passage helps you to capture the main idea of the passage you're reading. It is useful when you are collecting information or conducting research. Here are some guidelines for summarizing a passage.

First, read the passage through for its central theme, its tone and the type of writing it belongs to.

Second, read the passage again and closely for its main points and supporting points.

Third, write a one-sentence summary of each paragraph.

Fourth, write a short paragraph by combining the summary sentences of the paragraphs with any necessary changes to connect them.

Fifth, omit anything that is not related to the central theme and any illustrative examples and supporting details unless you find an example indispensable.

Sixth, be careful about different expressions for the same idea in the passage. The author may have expressed the same idea in different words for emphasis. However, there is no room for repetition of ideas in a summary.

At last, do not copy words and phrases from the passage. As far as possible the summary should be written in your own words.

Exercises

Please read the above reading skill of summarizing a whole passage and use the guidelines to summarize the passage in Short Passage One entitled "Can Online Courses Keep Students from Cheating?"

Summary: _____

_____

_____

_____

THINK

Academic Words in Use

Fill in the blanks in the following sentences with the appropriate words provided in the box below. Change the form of the words if necessary.

device	acknowledge	access	illustrative	founder	challenge
identification	approach	primary	registration	restrict	eliminate

1. Jack Ma, the _____ of Alibaba, makes great innovations in people's way of trading.

2. The _____ is fixed to a post.

3. The new government's first _____ is the economy.

4. The advantage of this _____ is that it retains the basic structure of the material.

5. At this stage, the security of our teams remains our _____ concern.

6. Students at the Belfast campus have _____ to excellent sports facilities.

7. He _____ that the purchase had been a mistake.

8. His only means of _____ was his passport.

9. He also encouraged countries across the region to work together to _____ poverty.

10. Ireland currently has some of the most _____ abortion laws in the world.

11. The example _____ how a simple financial process can create hundreds of thousands of dollars, with little money and low risk.

12. Go to the next window with this _____ form and the staff members there will tell you what other materials you will have to hand in.

Writing

For this part, you are allowed 30 minutes to read the following paragraphs and continue writing to make it a well-structured article. You should write at least 180 words but no more than 250 words.

Will E-Learning Replace Traditional Classrooms?

The meaning of traditional classrooms has changed over the years, especially with technology permeating some, then all, domains of the classroom environment. From projectors to smart screens and everything in between, technology has changed classroom learning as we know it. And now, online learning serves to switch up what we expect from learning environments, processes, and experiences.

As we can see, both online learning and classroom learning have their benefits. However, it is hard to see a clear vision of whether or not the classroom will be replaced.

Appendix: Video Script, Key and Sample Answers

Unit 1　Career Planning

Video script

The Fantasy, the Ideal, and the Reality of Career Exploration
NW: 525　GL: 6.7　AWL percentage: 6.69%　Duration: 3'38"　WPM: 146

You might fantasize that identifying your dream job will be easy. You might take a test to help you understand what you are good at and enjoy. The test works like a magic sorting hat: the best career pops out, you get a job, and are happy for the rest of your life! Or, you might take the idealized approach to your career exploration. You'd meet with a career counselor, and complete a self-assessment to identify the skills, tasks, and values you'd want in a job. Multiple possibilities come out. To narrow it down, you'd read about those careers, talk to professionals, fall in love with one career, and go get your dream job! This approach is linear and logical, but not usually what happens. In reality, career exploration is messy, laborious, and iterative.

Let's look at a typical case: a postdoc named John, ready to move on, but didn't know what he wanted to do. John met with a career counselor, took a self-assessment test, and a whole universe of career possibilities emerged! John narrowed his choices to three, and began investigating jobs as a management consultant, medical science liaison, and medical writer. He did some reading on consulting, and decided that consultants travel too much, so he eliminated that career. Next was medical science liaison. He liked what he read! He would be scientifically engaged while working with scientists and physicians. John talked to a medical science liaison, and liked most of what he heard, except that there are advancement ceilings, so he crossed that off the list. Move on to medical writing! Like before, John read and spoke with people. He liked what he learned! He especially liked that he wouldn't need previous experience. He was tired of his postdoc, and ready to make money! Over the course of a year, John applied for a ton of jobs, but got no interviews! Confused, he talked to more people. One told him that the field had changed. Now you needed experience! So, he took a $2,500 regulatory writing course that would make him competitive. Unfortunately, he hated it! By now, John was very frustrated, and told his sorry story to a classmate in the writing course. She suggested something different: Patent Agent. It seemed to involve the kinds of skills and tasks that John liked. This was an option he hadn't even considered! So he started the whole process over: reading and talking to people. This time, he also tested the work with a part-time internship at his university during his postdoc. He loved the work! He wrote reports, and met several patent agents and lawyers. One of them suggested that he take the patent bar; he did, and he passed! John applied for jobs, and found one quickly. These days, he's happily employed as a Senior Patent Agent at a biotech company. Career exploration is complicated, messy, and hard work! So start early; career exploration takes time! Don't rely on a single anecdote; get multiple data points! Embrace serendipity, because career leads can come from unexpected places! Try out the work in the low-risk way, and take heart. Eventually, everyone gets there!

Key and sample answers

Viewing

Understanding the video clip

$3 \to 2 \to 7 \to 5 \to 6 \to 4 \to 8 \to 1$

Further thoughts

Reasons for unemployment	Suggestions for job-hunters
1. Companies are more likely to choose the candidates with rich working experience.	1. It is advisable for colleges to adjust courses more closely related to the future jobs.
2. The current education system brings on a lot of bookworms who are adept in theoretical but not practical knowledge.	2. Students in college should not only get a good command of professional knowledge but also take part in some practical exercises to be prepared for the future jobs.
3. Proficient employees with rich and extensive working experience get retired at a much later age.	3. Government may stage laws and regulations to assist graduates in finding jobs. Don't be too worried about this.
...	...

Banked Cloze

1–5 EGACH 6–10 LOMBJ

Long Passage

1-5 FGIAM 6-10 CEKBH

Short Passages

Passage one 1-5 CDABC

Passage two 1-5 ADBDC

Reading Skills

1. six   2. early   3. well-equipped   4. employer perceptions

5. career readiness   6. resources   7. opportunities   8. Create

Academic Words in Use

1. recruitment   2. measurable   3. harshly   4. disproportionate

5. supportive   6. Unemployment   7. accomplishment   8. flourishing

9. competitive   10. convincing

Writing

Sample writing

Can Deciding on a Career Path Early Lead to a More Satisfying Life?

It is true that some people know from an early age what career they want to pursue, and they are happy to spend the rest of their lives in the same profession. While I admit that this may suit many people, I believe that others enjoy changing careers or seeking job satisfaction in different ways.

On the one hand, having a defined career path can certainly lead to a satisfying working life. First of all, settling down in only one career is extremely beneficial to building up critical working experience, and quickly becoming an expert in the field. Besides, experience on the job does help get promotion along with higher salary. Employers view loyal staff as a long-term investment, so promoting these staff within the company might serve their best interests.

On the other hand, people find happiness in their working lives in different ways. Not everyone dreams of doing a particular job, and it can be equally rewarding to try a variety of professions; starting out on a completely new career path can be a reinvigorating experience. In addition, job satisfaction is often the result of working conditions, rather than the career itself. For example, a positive working atmosphere, enthusiastic colleagues, and an inspirational boss can make working life much more satisfying, regardless of the profession.

In conclusion, it can certainly be satisfying to pursue a particular career for the whole of one's life, but this is by no means the only route to fulfillment.

Unit 2   Job-Hopping

Video script

The Secret to Being a Successful Freelancer

NW: 718   GL: 8.3   AWL percentage: 7.13%   Duration: 3′52″   WPM: 184

I used to be really bad at earning money. Early on, I was a junior financial planner, and my job was to help people manage their wealth. But my salary was so low that I started riding my bike to work to save money on gas, and I started a garden to save money on food. Now I run a bookkeeping agency that specifically serves creative businesses. This might sound strange coming from a former financial planner, but I'm not a fan of capitalism. Almost everyone I work with and know and love is an artist, including me. So I know, the way the system is set up, freelancers and artists are too often way underpaid. They often feel like focusing on money will corrupt their creativity, or they think they're just not that good at making money anyway. But the truth is, we can be good at it, and in fact, we have to be, because our freedom is at stake[1]: our freedom to create, to influence and to use the power of money to change the very exploitation that keeps artists broke to begin with. I'm not struggling anymore, and I've learned a lot since being a financial planner, and I just wanted to share that knowledge. So here's what I've learned and done.

---

1   at stake: 处于危险境地；处于成败关头

One: what you do. When it comes to your offer, you have to be able to answer the following question: why would anyone hire you over your competition? If you can't answer that question, neither can your potential clients, which means you can't charge more for the thing that makes your work special. Price becomes a differentiator, and bidding becomes a race to the bottom. What sets you apart could be what you do, why you do it or how you do it: a string quartet[2] that arranges and plays hip-hop medleys, or a branding firm that has a unique way of marketing technology to Baby Boomers, or a prop and set designer who's known for crafting beautiful papier-mâché miniatures.[3]

Two: who you do it for. After you determine what sets you apart, position yourself for your ideal customer. In order for this to be effective, you must narrow your focus. Without focus, you try to be everything for everyone, and you end up being nothing for nobody. Then, use the kind of language that appeals to your target customer. Create the kind of marketing materials or the kind of portfolio that attracts them. Then, be in the real-life and virtual places they are. For example, if you're a videographer and you want to work with mission-driven companies that bring clean water to places where it's scarce, create a video trailer that shows exactly how the power of film moves people to act.

Three: when it's time to talk money, understand the real value that you create. You're not just being compensated for the time that you work on a project. You're being compensated for everything you've learned and everything you've done over the years that make you excellent at what you do. Ask yourself questions like: how does your service impact a customer's bottom line? How do you create efficiencies that generate cost savings? How much money can your customer make from a product that you helped them create? For example, if you're a freelancer that helps YouTube creators develop merch like T-shirts and dad hats, mention how much money you've helped your clients generate. Or, if you've created a diversity and inclusion training program for corporations, talk about how much time and money a company saves purchasing your product instead of developing their own.

Four: make sure your price includes your taxes, your overhead and your profit. When you're a freelancer, you are your own business, so you're responsible for marketing, accounting, taxes, legal, insurance, overhead and profit. If you price too low, you've already negotiated against yourself. And if a potential customer balks at your pricing, don't apologize. Just say that you're running a business and you can't afford to do the work for less. Instead of corrupting your creativity, focusing on making more money could actually enhance it by giving you the freedom of choice. Because when you earn enough working with clients that value your work, you don't have to compromise by working with clients who don't.

---

2 string quartet: 弦乐四重奏乐团
3 papier-mâché miniatures: 用混合纸制作的手工艺品

Key and sample answers

Viewing

Understanding the video clip

Filling in the blanks

Four tips by the speaker	Details
What you do.	When it comes to your offer, you have to be able to answer the following question: why would anyone hire you over your competition?
Who you do it for.	After you determine what sets you apart, position yourself for your ideal customer. In order for this to be effective, you must narrow your focus.
When it's time to talk money, understand the real value that you create.	You're not just being compensated for the time that you work on a project. Ask yourself questions like: How does your service impact a customer's bottom line?
Make sure your price includes your taxes, your overhead and your profit.	When you're a freelancer, you are your own business.

Ture of false

1-5 TFTFT

Banked Cloze

1-5 BHFKA   6-10 ELMCO

Long Passage

1-5 AFJPH   6-10 NIESC

Short Passages

Passage one 1-5 BDAAC
Passage two 1-5 BCDAD

Reading Skills

1. The topic of this paragraph is <u>job-hopping</u>.

2. The main idea of this paragraph is <u>"Employers and recruiters' attitude towards job-hopping used to be unsupportive, yet they begin to have a different outlook now."</u>

3. Hiring managers' attitude towards job-hopping used to be <u>wary/cautious/unsupportive</u>, but now they <u>have changed their attitude/begin to have a different outlook</u>.

4. The topic sentence of this paragraph is <u>"Younger workers remain more wedded to their current jobs than they were before the recession."</u>

5. <u>The author supports the idea of the topic sentence in this paragraph by referring to the idea of an expert in this area—Neil Carberry.</u>

6. The topic sentence of this paragraph is <u>"teenagers can hardly be expected to have an in-depth knowledge of the minutiae of labour-market trends."</u>

Academic Words in Use

1. recruited   2. dampen   3. resume   4. Unemployment   5. mismatch

6. recession   7. identify   8. professional   9. boosted   10. longevity

Writing

Sample writing

Factors You Should Consider while Changing Your Job

Switching a job is not an easy task. One has to think about a number of aspects in order to reach any particular conclusion. Avoid taking any decision in a hurry because once you quit a job, the action is irreversible. There are important factors that you need to consider before making this career move.

Why do you want to change careers?

Knowing why you're doing something helps you stay focused and make better decisions. Get clear on the reasons why you want to make that change happen and take the time to think things through. For example, how will taking a new job now benefit you in the future? Is there something specific about your current job that's driving you to want to make a change? Have you been in the same field for a while and want to try something new? Once you know your "why", it's time to figure out just how big of a change you're looking to make.

How much are you prepared to change?

Think about all of the factors that go into making that change. Things like time spent learning a new profession, the possibility of having to start out in a lower role than you're currently in, and the learning curve of being in a new industry are all important factors to consider. Also consider the factors outside of work. Think about a new job or career's impact on your personal life. Your personal life and your work life should be able to coexist with each other.

What direction do you want your career to take?

The main point of making a career change is to keep moving forward. A new career must help you achieve your professional goals.

Unit 3   Financial Management

Video script

How to Manage Your Student Loans

NW: 339   GL: 11.9   AWL percentage: 7.31%   Duration: 2′27″   WPM: 138

If you have a federal student loan, there are several options available to help you manage your debt. And if you're having trouble making your loan payments, contact your loan servicer immediately. Your loan servicer will walk you through your options. For example, you might consider changing your repayment plan. There are several repayment options available to you. Most borrowers start off with the standard repayment plan, which offers a fixed payment over a 10-year period. However, you can lower your initial monthly payments using a graduated repayment plan that starts with lower monthly payments that gradually increase over time. Or if you qualify, you may be able to lower your monthly payments by extending them over a longer period of time. Finally, you may be able to choose a repayment plan that ties your monthly payments to your income. If you meet certain requirements, you may be able to defer or temporarily postpone your payments for a variety of reasons, including a return to school, unemployment, or military service. If you're having trouble making your loan payments, but do not qualify for a deferment, your loan servicer may grant forbearance, which allows you to postpone or reduce your monthly payment for a limited period of time due to financial difficulty or certain other reasons. Contact your loan servicer to see if you qualify for deferment or forbearance. If you have multiple federal loans, consolidating them into one loan may also help you better manage your debt. In addition to having to make only one federal student loan payment each month, your monthly payment amount may be lower since the length of your repayment schedule may be extended. Consolidating your loans is easy and can be done any time after you leave school. Switching repayment plans, exploring deferment and forbearance options, or consolidating your loans may help you better manage your student loan payments and avoid default. Remember, if you're having difficulty making payments, contact your loan servicer immediately to discuss the pros and cons of these options.

Key and sample answers

Viewing

Understanding the video clip

Problems that you may encounter	Possible solutions
1. If you're having trouble making your loan payments,	contact your loan servicer immediately.
2. If you qualify,	you may be able to lower your monthly payments by extending them over a longer period of time.
3. If you meet certain requirements,	you may be able to defer or temporarily postpone your payments.
4. If you do not qualify for a deferment,	your loan servicer may grant forbearance.
5. If you have multiple federal loans,	you can consolidate them into one loan.

Further thoughts

Benefits of student loans	Drawbacks of student loans
1. With the loan, student borrowers can pay the tuition and support their life on the campus.	1. Student borrowers might be very anxious because of the debt.
2. With the loan, student borrowers will not depend on their parents.	2. Student borrowers may feel self-abased.
3. With the loan, student borrowers will be encouraged to save money and develop good financial habits.	3. Student borrowers have to face great financial pressure after graduation.

Banked Cloze

1-5 KBIAG   6-10 ECDLN

Long Passage

1-5 GEKBL   6-10 IHDMF

Short Passages

Passage one 1-5 DCABB

Passage two 1-5 CAABD

Reading Skills

Paragraph D: Budget for everything.

Paragraph E: Purchase used schoolbooks and sell your old ones.

Paragraph F: Automate your savings.

Paragraph G: Get creative and find fun for free.

Paragraph H: Steer clear of automated payments.

Academic Words in Use

1. accessible   2. behavioral   3. maintenance   4. recognition   5. commercial

6. cancellation 7. automated   8. initiative   9. overwhelming   10. devastating

Writing

Sample writing

Is the Wide Use of Private Cars More Destructive or Constructive?

Nowadays, the number of private cars is consistently on the rise. Obviously, a car owner is offered a more flexible schedule than those who rely on public transportation. Apart from that, being more mobile is considered as another big advantage. However, the prevalence of private cars has brought about many a problem that cannot be neglected.

First, the popularization of vehicles poses heavy threats to the environment. To start with, with current technology, the more energy is consumed, the more air pollution is generated. Cars drink up huge amounts of fuel and throw out huge amounts of pollutants. As a result, these poisonous particles seriously destroy the atmosphere, which renders the air of cities, metropolis in particular, unbearable.

Second, noise pollution is also closely associated with the alarming growing volume of traffic worldwide. It is reported that noise originating from traffic transportation accounts for 75% among all the city noise. Without doubt, cars are the chief culprit. The noise around the downtown of a city will inevitably influence citizens' routine life and work.

In addition, for every family, owning a car is a big expense. Apart from fuel, tolls, insurance, car repair and maintenance costs will amount to a big sum of money, which is a great burden to an average family.

To sum up, instead of comfort and convenience the fantastic spur of auto industry brings about to individuals, it incurs heavy risks to the surroundings that we rely on. Therefore, I firmly believe that the wide use of cars is more destructive than constructive.

Unit 4　Why Do We Travel?

Video script

The Point of Travel

NW: 501　GL: 8.9　AWL percentage: 1.95%　Duration: 3′06″　WPM: 162

What's the point of travel? It's to help make us into better people. It's a sort of therapy. Without anything mystical being meant by this, all of us are, in one way or another, on what could be termed "an inner journey." That is, we're trying to develop in particular ways. In a nutshell, the point of travel is to go to places that can help us in our inner evolution. The outer journey should assist us with the inner one. Every location in the world contains qualities that can support some kind of beneficial change inside a person. Take these 200-million-year-old stones in America's Utah Desert. It's a place, but looked at psychologically, it's also an inner destination, a place with perspective, free of preoccupation with the petty and the small-minded, somewhere imbued with calm and resilience. Religions used to take travel much more seriously than we do now. For them, it was a therapeutic activity. In the Middle Ages, when there was something wrong with you, you were meant to head out for a pilgrimage to commune with relics of a saint or a member of the holy family. If you had toothache, you'd go to Rome, to the Basilica of San Lorenzo[1] and touch the arm bones of Saint Appolonia, the patron saint of teeth. If you were unhappily married, you might go to Umbria to touch the shrine of Saint Rita of Cascia, patron saint of marital problems. Or, if you were worried about lightning, you were sent to Bad Münstereifel[2] in Germany to touch the skull of Saint Donatus, believed to offer help against fires and explosions. We no longer believe in the divine power of journeys, but certain parts of the world still have a power to change and mend the wounded parts of us. In an ideal world, travel agencies would be manned by a new kind of psychotherapist. They'd take care not just of the flights and the hotels; they'd start by finding out what was wrong with us and how we might want to change. The anxious might be sent to see the majestic, immemorial waves crashing into the cliffs on the west coast of Ireland. People a bit too concerned with being admired and famous might be sent to contemplate the ruins of Detroit. Someone out of touch with their body might be recommended a trip to Porto Seguro[3] in Bahia in Brazil. Nowadays, too often, we head off without fully knowing what's wrong with us or precisely understanding how our chosen destinations meant to help us. We should become more conscious travelers on a well-articulated search for qualities

---

1　Basilica of San Lorenzo: 圣洛伦佐大教堂
2　Bad Münstereifel: 德国的一个小镇
3　Porto Seguro: 巴西的塞古罗港

that places possess, like calm or perspective, sensuality or rigor. We should follow old-fashioned pilgrims in striving to evolve our characters according to the suggestions offered up by the places we've been to. We need to relearn how to be ambitious about travel, seeing it as a way of helping us to grow into better versions of ourselves.

Key and sample answers

Viewing

Understanding the video clip

1. inner	2. beneficial	3. preoccupation	4. commune
5. wounded	6. contemplate	7. conscious	8. versions

Further thoughts

Business travel is necessary	Business travel is unnecessary
1. To attend an exhibition or trade fair in a different region or even a different country will promote success.	1. As e-commerce can handle everything, there is no need to travel.
2. To meet business partners face to face will improve the probability of collaboration.	2. Business travel is a waste of time and money.

Banked Cloze

1-5 BDHAI   6-10 CKNEL

Long Passage

1-5 JBDKG   6-10 ACIHF

Short Passages

Passage one 1-5 CAADB
Passage two 1-5 CABCD

Reading Skills

2 → 4 → 1 → 6 → 5 → 3

Academic Words in Use

1. anxiety 2. flexibility 3. unimaginable 4. potentially 5. invulnerable

6. empowered 7. compassionate 8. enthusiastic 9. isolated 10. contribution

Writing

Sample writing

Is It Necessary to Travel Abroad to Learn about Foreign Countries?

Some people think that it is necessary to travel abroad to learn about other countries, but other people think that it is not necessary to travel abroad because all the information can be seen on TV and the Internet. I would argue that it is still of necessity to visit the nations to fully learn about them.

There is no denying that nowadays live videos and international television channels can provide first-hand information about the life in foreign countries. However, although watching videos and reading blogs are convenient, one cannot learn enough until he experiences it in the real life. It's just like that you cannot learn a language only by reading books and listening to tutorials. A pragmatic approach, such as interacting with native speakers, is required. There's nothing quite like walking along the Champs Elysees in Paris or the Fifth Avenue in New York in person. You won't really appreciate the amazing beach of Santa Monica until you see it with your own eyes. You can read all the books in the world about the pyramids in Egypt or the Louvre, but being there is a different story.

In conclusion, despite the availability of information and resources on the Internet to learn about any foreign destination, I firmly believe that physical presence is required to have a deep understanding about foreign cultures.

Unit 5　Being Friendly to the Environment

Causes and Effects of Climate Change

NW: 367　GL: 10.2　AWL percentage: 6.5%　Duration: 3′04″　WPM: 118

Human activities, from pollution to overpopulation, are driving up the earth's temperature and fundamentally changing the world around us. The main cause is a phenomenon known as the greenhouse effect. Gases in the atmosphere, such as water vapor, carbon dioxide, methane, nitrous oxide, and chlorofluorocarbons, let the sun's light in, but keep some of the heat from escaping, like the glass walls of a greenhouse. The more greenhouse gases in the atmosphere, the more heat gets trapped, strengthening the greenhouse effect and increasing the earth's temperature. Human activities, like the burning of fossil fuels, have increased the amount of CO_2 in the atmosphere by more than a third since the Industrial Revolution. The rapid increase in greenhouse gases in the atmosphere has warmed the planet at an alarming rate. While Earth's climate has fluctuated in the past, atmospheric carbon dioxide hasn't reached today's levels in hundreds of thousands of years. Climate change has consequences for our oceans, our weather, our food sources, and our health. Ice sheets, such as Greenland and Antarctica, are melting. The extra water that was once held in Glaciers causes sea levels to rise and spills out of the oceans, flooding coastal regions. Warmer temperatures also make weather more extreme. This means not only more intense major storms, floods and heavy snowfall, but also longer and more frequent droughts. These changes in weather pose challenges. Growing crops becomes more difficult, the areas where plants and animals can live shift, and water supplies are diminished. In addition to creating new agricultural challenges, climate change can directly affect people's physical health. In urban areas, the warmer atmosphere creates an environment that traps and increases the amount of smog. This is because smog contains ozone particles, which increase rapidly at higher temperatures. Exposure to higher levels of smog can cause health problems, such as asthma, heart disease and lung cancer. While the rapid rate of climate change is caused by humans, humans are also the ones who can combat it. If we work to replace fossil fuels with renewable energy sources like solar and wind, which don't produce greenhouse gas emissions, we might still be able to prevent some of the worst effects of climate change.

Key and sample answers

Viewing

Understanding the video clip

Causes	Effects
1. pollution and overpopulation	fundamentally changing the world
2. greenhouse gases in the atmosphere	increasing the earth's temperature
3. the burning of fossil fuels	increasing the amount of CO_2
4. climate change	melting ice sheets
5. the rise of sea levels	flooding coastal regions
6. exposure to higher levels of smog	health problems (asthma, heart disease and lung cancer)

Further thoughts

We can do the following things to protect the environment:

1. recycle newspapers and bottles;

2. take public transport to get to work;

3. turn off lights when going out;

4. maintain the air conditioning temperature at 26 degree in hot summer;

5. plant more trees;

6. try to buy locally produced fruit and vegetables.

Banked Cloze

1-5 KDABC　6-10 NLIJG

Long Passage

1-5 MBEKD　6-10 LGFNC

Short Passages

Passage one 1-5 BDCAD
Passage two 1-5 DBCDA

Reading Skills

1. To inform.

2. To persuade.

3. To inform.

4. To persuade.

5. To persuade.

6. To persuade.

7. To entertain.

8. To inform.

Academic Words in Use

1. unsustainable   2. available   3. harmonious   4. Consumption

5. globally   6. disregard   7. inconsistent   8. integration

9. contamination   10. resolution

Writing

Sample writing

Should We Spend Our Time and Energy
Protecting Wild Animals or Human Beings?

In these days, with some improper human activities such as hunting rare animals and the extinction of some endangered animals, there has been an intense debate about whether too many resources, including time and money, should be allocated to preserve wild animals.

Proponents of this opinion may argue that human beings could have done more to safeguard wild animals from being extinct, so that less animals would have died out or diminished. After all, animals, as a key component of the whole food chain, exert a profound impact on the sustainability of an ecosystem. If the importance of protecting wildlife is underestimated, we human beings would be affected adversely in the end.

However, considering the allocation of the taxes levied from citizens, opponents believe that the government has more issues related to human rather than animals to give priority to, among which are education and technology, and there is no doubt that these two aspects are essential for human further development economically and environmentally. As a result, the two industries give an impetus to the economic development of society, which will be conducive to the protection of wildlife in turn.

From my perspective, considerable significance should be attached to the preservation of wildlife, but in the meantime, other crucial projects should not be ignored, especially education and technology.

Unit 6   Internet and Life

Video script

What Is Cloud Computing?

NW: 418   GL: 14.1   AWL percentage: 11%   Duration: 3′11″   WPM: 131

Cloud computing is the on-demand delivery of IT resources via the Internet, with pay-as-you-go pricing. Instead of buying, owning and maintaining physical data centers and servers, you can access technology services, such as computing power, storage and databases, on an as-needed basis from a Cloud provider like Amazon Web Services. Organizations of every type, size and industry are using the Cloud for a wide variety of use cases, such as data backup, disaster recovery, email, virtual desktops, software development and testing, big data analytics, and customer facing web applications. For example, health care companies are using the Cloud to develop more personalized treatments for patients. Financial services companies are using the Cloud to power real-time fraud detection and prevention. And video game makers are using the Cloud to deliver online games to millions of players around the world. With Cloud computing your business can become more agile, reduce costs, instantly scale, and deploy globally in minutes. Cloud computing gives you instance access to a broad range of technologies, so you can innovate faster and build nearly anything you can imagine, from infrastructure services such as compute, storage and databases, to Internet of Things, machine learning, data analytics and much more. You can deploy technology services in a matter of minutes and get from idea to implementation several orders of magnitude faster than before. This gives you the freedom to experiment and test new ideas to differentiate customer experiences and transform your business, such as adding machine learning and intelligence to your applications in order to personalize experiences for your customers and improve their engagement. You don't need to make large, upfront investments in hardware and overpay for capacity you don't use. Instead, you can trade capital expense for variable expense and only pay for IT as you consume it. With Cloud computing you access resources from the Cloud in real time as they're needed. You can scale these resources up and down to grow or shrink capacity instantly as your business needs change. Cloud computing also makes it easy to expand to new regions and deploy globally in minutes. For example, Amazon Web Services has infrastructure all over the world, so you're able to deploy your application in multiple physical locations in just a few clicks. Putting applications in closer proximity to end users reduces latency and improves their experience. No matter your location, size or industry, the Cloud frees you from managing infrastructure and data centers, so you can focus on what matters most to your business.

Key and sample answers

Viewing

Understanding the video clip

Filling in the blanks

1. Cloud computing is the on-demand <u>delivery of IT resources via the Internet</u>, with pay-as-you-go pricing.

2. Organizations of every type, size and industry are using the Cloud for a wide variety of use cases, such as data backup, <u>disaster recovery</u>, email, <u>virtual desktops</u>, software development and testing, <u>big data analytics</u>, and customer facing web applications.

3. With Cloud computing your business can become <u>more agile, reduce costs, instantly scale,</u> and deploy globally in minutes.

4. You can <u>deploy technology services</u> in a matter of minutes and <u>get from idea to implementation</u> several orders of magnitude faster than before.

   This gives you the freedom to experiment and test new ideas to <u>differentiate customer experiences</u> and transform your business.

Matching

Health care companies are using the Cloud	to develop more <u>personalized treatments</u> for patients.
Financial services companies are using the Cloud	to power real-time fraud <u>detection and prevention</u>.
Video game makers are using the Cloud	to deliver <u>online games</u> to millions of players around the world.

Banked Cloze

1-5 CBEHD   6-10 JNIAL

Long Passage

1-5 QBLKP   6-10 UFCHI

Short Passages

Passage one 1-5 BDCBB
Passage two 1-5 CBADC

Reading Skills

1. The author of this article is Tim Berners-Lee. He invented the World Wide Web. He is co-founder of the World Wide Web Foundation and chief technology officer at Inrupt. Since he is the leading expert in the Internet area, he is qualified to write about this topic.

2. The author wants to advocate that the government and the individuals should pay attention to the problem of inequitable access to Internet highlighted by the COVID-19 pandemic and strive to achieve universal Internet access.

3. The article argues that though online reviews theoretically should be helping the users make good decisions about what to buy, yet they actually don't always help us make best decisions. I agree with the view since I think we tend to easily fall into herd mentality mindset and choose to purchase more popular products.

Academic Words in Use

1. addicted   2. outlined   3. affordable   4. universal   5. mentality

6. withdrew   7. reviews   8. network   9. access   10. inclined

Writing

Sample writing

Does the Internet Help or Hurt Social Interaction?

In modern society, people tend to spend burgeoning amount of time on the Internet than with others. Some people worry that this technology impedes people's communication skills, while others feel that the Internet gives individual greater opportunities to connect with people all over the world.

The Internet can have a negative impact on communication. One reason for this is the amount of time some people spend online. Many teenagers spend hours after hours in front of their computers, instead of mixing with others or engaging in more social activities. Consequently, they are inclined to have fewer time to meet others and might inadvertently start to ignore acquaintances, friends or even family members.

On the other hand, the Internet can be used for social interaction. E-mail, for instance, enables people to correspond with each other quickly and conveniently. It is a much better medium for communication than letters because it is instant. Therefore, people can use it on a daily basis to keep in contact with family and friends. MSN is another facility that aids communication. People can use it to send messages back and forth. Recently, Skype has become popular. It allows you to use your computer like a telephone to talk with anyone around the world. The above-mentioned uses show that the Internet can be a useful communication tool.

In conclusion, although some people spend too much time doing uncommunicative activities online, most people use the Internet to increase their opportunities to interact with others. So, on the whole, the Internet is good for communication.

Unit 7　Where Do You Want to Work?

Video script

More People Considering Moving Out of Expensive Cities
if They Can Work Remotely

NW: 389　GL: 8.0　AWL percentage: 3%　Duration: 2′33″　WPM: 153

Big cities may be losing some of their luster thanks to the corona virus pandemic. Companies are going to be working remotely long after this pandemic. With so many companies like Google, Facebook, Dell and Walmart allowing employees to work from home for good, and social distancing the new norm, many city residents are eyeing greener pastures. Sales manager Jared Schwartz and his wife Kim have been working, living and educating their eight-year-old son Tyler in a small Manhattan apartment during stay at home orders about three months now, prompting them to ask why pay so much for so little. "We don't necessarily want to escape New York City, but yes, moving on and looking to get somewhere where we can carry on with a more normal life style." The Schwartzs are not alone. Moves out of New York City to Connecticut, for example, have more than doubled since April. And a new national survey by Zillow found 2/3 of people would consider moving if their jobs let them telework from home as often as they liked. The Schwartzs have that flexibility so they're packing up and moving to suburban Nashville, buying their new house without ever having seen it in person. "You've seen it through FaceTime and you have a trustworthy realtor, but it's a gamble and more ways than one, right?" "It is absolutely the most stressful part of all of this. It's… having not actually seen it in person, so you get a lot of inspections and hope it's working in order." It's a good time to move with mortgage rates hitting an all-time low, making buying more affordable. The bottom line is about the cost of living. The median home price in the New York and New Jersey area is four hundred twenty-four thousand dollars, around Nashville two hundred and seventy-five thousand. And realtor Belle Guzman says when you're living and working in your house, extra space matters even more. "Home, that's really taken on a whole new meaning when we look at the way people are using it today. It becomes your gym, your office, your schoolroom, your restaurant. It's really become a significant part of who we are and how we're living." And changing where we really feel at home. For today Jolene Kent NBC News Los Angeles.

Viewing

Understanding the video clip

Filling in the blanks

1. Companies are going to be working <u>remotely</u> long after this pandemic.

2. With so many <u>companies</u> like Google, Facebook, Dell and Walmart allowing employees to work from home <u>for good</u>, and social distancing the new norm, many city residents are <u>eyeing</u> greener pastures.

3. Moves out of New York City to Connecticut, for example, have <u>more than doubled</u> since April.

4. The median home price in the New York and New Jersey area is <u>424,000</u> dollars, around Nashville <u>275,000</u>.

5. When you're living and working in your house, <u>extra space</u> matters even more.

Marking

Reasons why people are considering moving out of expensive cities	Mentioned or not
1. Many companies like Google, Facebook, Dell and Walmart allow employees to work from home for some time.	×
2. The median home price in small cities is much cheaper than the big cities	√
3. Many people necessarily want to escape big cities like New York City.	×
4. When you're living and working in your house, extra space matters even more.	√
5. It's a good time to move with mortgage rates hitting an all-time low, making buying more affordable.	√

Banked Cloze

1-5 DBOHC 6-10 AJFKM

Long Passage

1-5 DPNOJ 6-10 BLAGH

Short Passages

Passage one 1-5 BCCDB

Passage two 1-5 BCCDA

Reading Skills

Annotations	Paragraph

1. <u>flexibility</u>
    n. the ability to change or be changed easily to suit a different situation
2. <u>opt</u>
    v. to choose one thing or do one thing instead of another
3. The factor influencing her choice for a smaller city in-between both sets of grandparents:
    "<u>with two young children and a spouse who could work from anywhere…</u>"
4. This was as much a <u>professional</u> move as a <u>personal</u> one.
5. The outcome of her choice of working location:
    "<u>she could travel more and work more unpredictable hours…</u>"
	2 - How important is where you live versus other factors?
	An HR colleague of mine actually did have the flexibility to move and ultimately did move. She was in the finance industry in NYC, so arguably the global capital for her career path, but with two young children and a spouse who could work from anywhere, she opted for a smaller city in-between both sets of grandparents. This was as much a professional move as a personal one. With the additional nearby resources, she could travel more and work more unpredictable hours, which enabled her to take a bigger role than what she initially had. (Extracted from Long Passage in this unit)

Academic Words in Use

1. high-skilled   2. talents   3. career   4. innovations   5. executive

6. flexibility   7. adjust   8. commitment   9. revolutionized   10. envisions

Writing

Sample writing

Should a Career Be Started in a Big City or a Small City?

It's easy to be attracted to the idea of a big city—fast-paced, brightly-lit—the perfect setting for one's burning ambitions. But what if moving to the big city isn't the only way to find success? In fact, small cities and regional areas can also have advantages for one's career.

First of all, smaller areas are more likely to have a shortage of qualified professionals, which can help a specialist shine. If one finds it is difficult to stand out in a big city, considering moving to a smaller place instead may present an opportunity.

Secondly, smaller cities tend to have lower costs. Money is always the stumbling block to starting a business and commercial rents can be one of the biggest line items for a new business. Rents in a small city are usually lower, helping enterprises relieve their economic pressure to some extent.

Finally, it is easier to build a personal connection with others in small places. In a small city, the relationship between people is closer. Fully tapped personal connections may contribute to one's career development.

Unit 8   Online Education

Video script

Common Misconceptions about Distance Learning

NW: 684   GL: 9.6   AWL percentage: 7.13%   Duration: 4′38″   WPM: 149

Welcome to the world of distance learning. In this video, we will discuss the seven common misconceptions students have about distance learning.

1. Online classes are easier than traditional classes. You think that an online class would be easier than a traditional course. Actually, online courses are just as hard or even more challenging than traditional courses. For example, in addition to typical classroom activities like readings, test, and papers, online courses also have interactive assignments, such as discussion board postings, collaborative projects, and game-based activities. This work will be frequent, and may feel more challenging for you to accomplish. Whereas face-to-face courses might meet just two times a week and require little participation, online courses often require students to complete activities almost daily, and all students will be required to contribute.

2. Online courses take less time than traditional courses. You think it will take less time because you don't have to sit in the classroom. The reality is that an online course can take as much or more time as a traditional course. You will be expected to check your email frequently, get all assignments done on time, discuss your questions and concerns with your instructor and classmates, and fully participate each week. Therefore, don't expect to succeed in an online course just by logging into the course once per week. Instead, log in frequently and stay engaged to keep yourself on the right track.

3. I can work entirely at my own pace. Flexibility is considered one of the greatest advantages of online learning, but this does not mean you can work entirely at your own pace. Online classes still have deadlines. In courses with synchronous meetings and discussions, you'll have to show up at specific times or places to participate, thus you'll need to be a self-starter and you'll need to manage your time well. If you can do that, then you'll enjoy how flexible online learning can be.

4. I won't get to know the other students very well in an online course. While you may never meet your instructors or peers in person, good online courses help you develop similar relationships to those you have in face-to-face courses. For instance, icebreakers and self-introductions give you the opportunity to learn about each other, discussion board activities and collaborative assignments create opportunities for you to be engaged with each other in significant mutually supportive ways. If you feel shy in a face-to-face classroom, you may even have an easier time connecting with other students in an online class.

5. I won't get individual attention from my professor. This could not be farther from the truth. In online courses, your professors will participate in your classroom discussions, hold virtual office hours, and give feedback for each homework submission, just as they would in a traditional classroom. You will have access to help when you need it. Don't be afraid to speak up for yourself. Initiate a conversation with you professor and let them know when you're having difficulties.

6. I won't learn as much in an online course. Good online courses can accomplish the same student learning outcomes as traditional face-to-face courses with high levels of engagement.

7. Online degrees don't carry the respect of traditional college degrees. Because the online curriculum is the same that you would learn in campus-based courses and shares the same prestigious accreditation, the only difference is the delivery. In fact, more students are choosing to pursue their degrees online due to the flexibility of the format.

So, let's put it all together. Here is what we've learned. Online courses are as hard, or more challenging than traditional courses. Online courses take as much or more time than face-to-face courses. Taking an online class does not mean that you can work entirely at your own pace. You'll have opportunities to get to know your classmates in the online learning environment. You can still get individual attention and help from your professors. You can achieve the same learning outcomes in an online class as a traditional face-to-face class. Online degrees carry the respect of traditional college degrees.

Viewing

Understanding the video clip

Misconceptions	Realities
1. Online classes are easier than traditional classes.	Online courses are as hard or even more challenging than traditional courses. For example, in addition to typical classroom activities like readings, test, and papers, online courses also have <u>interactive assignments</u>, such as discussion board postings, collaborative projects, and game-based activities. Whereas face-to-face courses might meet just two times a week and require <u>little participation</u>, online courses often require students to complete activities <u>almost daily</u>, and all students will be required to contribute.
2. Online courses take less time than traditional courses.	The reality is that an online course can take <u>as much or more</u> time as a traditional course. You need to log in frequently and stay engaged to keep yourself <u>on the right track</u>.
3. I can work entirely at my own pace.	Online classes still <u>have deadlines</u>. You'll have to show up at specific times or places to participate, thus you'll need to be <u>a self-starter</u> and you'll need to manage your time well.
4. I won't get to know the other students very well in an online course.	Good online courses help you develop similar relationships to those you have in face-to-face courses. Through icebreakers, self-introductions, <u>discussion board activities</u> and collaborative assignments you will get to know your classmates well. If you feel shy in a face-to-face classroom, you may even have an easier time <u>connecting with</u> other students in an online class.
5. I won't get individual attention from my professor.	You will have access to help when you need it. Initiate a conversation with you professor and let them know when you're <u>having difficulties</u>.
6. I won't learn as much in an online course.	Good online courses can accomplish the same <u>student learning outcomes</u> as traditional face-to-face courses with high levels of engagement.
7. Online degrees don't carry the respect of traditional college degrees.	Online curriculum is the same that you would learn in campus-based courses and shares the same prestigious accreditation, the only difference is <u>the delivery</u>.

Further thoughts

Benefits of distance learning	Drawbacks of distance learning
1. It's flexible.	1. It is difficult to stay motivated.
2. It improves computer skills.	2. It has no physical interaction.
3. It is less expensive.	3. Students can be easily distracted when learning from home.
4. Its courses can be customized.	4. It is unfriendly for students with limited access to technologies.
5. It is less threatening for introvert students.	5. It is difficult to prevent cheating.

Banked Cloze

1-5 NJMLA   6-10 CDIBE

Long Passage

1-5 CEIHD   6-10 JGLMK

Short Passages

Passage one 1-5 ADABC
Passage two 1-5 BDCCA

Reading Skills

Summary: MOOC providers have been fighting cheating for a long time, but they are unable to eradicate cheating with many tactics being employed. And if MOOC providers spend too much energy and money on cracking down on cheating, it will run counter to the original purpose of MOOCs and make them lose too much of their openness.

Academic Words in Use

1. founder   2. device   3. challenge   4. approach   5. primary

6. access   7. acknowledged   8. identification   9. eliminate   10. restrictive

11. illustrates   12. registration

Writing

Sample writing

Will E-Learning Replace Traditional Classrooms?

The meaning of traditional classrooms has changed over the years, especially with technology permeating some, then all, domains of the classroom environment. From projectors to smart screens and everything in between, technology has changed classroom learning as we know it. And now, online learning serves to switch up what we expect from learning environments, processes, and experiences.

As we can see, both online learning and classroom learning have their benefits. However, it is hard to see a clear vision of whether or not the classroom will be replaced.

E-learning tools provide educators and students with access to resources they couldn't have had otherwise, no matter their status or location. A philosophy student in England can learn from the top professor a continent away, and can do so in their own time while balancing a full-time job and a family at home.

But even though e-learning has become an education equalizer, it's still not a replacement for the traditional classroom. Sure, as technology is getting increasingly better every day, we may see changes to learning environments, but technology is not flawless. Just like any new, burgeoning innovation, e-learning faces its own challenges.

This, to me, is where e-learning and the traditional classroom will one day form a union: compensating for one where the other lacks.